MAIN LIBRARY

ACPL ITEM
DISCARDED

658.1512 C36p 2280509
Chang, Lucia S.
The perceived usefulness of
financial statements...

DO NOT REMOVE
CARDS FROM POCKET

ALLEN COUNTY PUBLIC LIBRARY

FORT WAYNE, INDIANA 46802

You may return this book to any agency, branch,
or bookmobile of the Allen County Public Library.

DEMCO

The Perceived Usefulness of Financial Statements for Investors' Decisions

Lucia S. Chang
and
Kenneth S. Most

University Presses of Florida
Florida International University Press
Miami

© 1985 by the Board of Regents of the State of Florida
All rights reserved.

Printed in U.S.A. on acid-free paper.

Allen County Public Library
Ft. Wayne, Indiana

Library of Congress Cataloging in Publication Data

Chang, Lucia S.
The perceived usefulness of financial statements for investors' decisions.

1. Financial statements. 2. Corporation reports.
I. Most, Kenneth S. II. Title.
HF5681.B2C42 1985 658.1'512 84-25788
ISBN 0-8130-0752-6 (alk. paper)

University Presses of Florida is the central agency for scholarly publishing of the State of Florida's university system, producing books selected for publication by the faculty editorial committees of Florida's nine public universities: Florida A & M University (Tallahassee), Florida Atlantic University (Boca Raton), Florida International University (Miami), Florida State University (Tallahassee), University of Central Florida (Orlando), University of Florida (Gainesville), University of North Florida (Jacksonville), University of South Florida (Tampa), University of West Florida (Pensacola).

Orders for books published by all member presses of University Presses of Florida should be addressed to University Presses of Florida, 15 NW 15th Street, Gainesville, FL 32603.

:: Contents

2280509

:: Tables

:: Acknowledgments

This book summarizes the findings of a study which has occupied much of our time since 1976.

We are grateful to the Florida International University Foundation for the research grant that enabled us to start this project. We thank Dr. Carlos W. Brain of Florida International University for extensive assistance in the development of the statistical tests of our data. We thank also Professors Ali C. Osman, of the Polytechnic of North London, and William J. Cotton, of the University of Canterbury in New Zealand, for the major contribution they made to this project by conducting part of the research in the United Kingdom and New Zealand.

Several Florida International University students provided valuable help with the computer runs and laying out the tables. We thank particularly Eduardo Caso, Carol Hill, and Marilyn Struby in this connection.

Finally, we thank Dr. Thomas Breslin and the members of the Florida International University Research and Publications Committee for their encouragement and assistance in bringing this work to publication.

Lucia S. Chang
Kenneth S. Most

1 :: The Usefulness of Financial Statements

Major changes in business finance during the past decade have led to debate and controversy on the meaning and objectives of financial reporting. Since the publication of the Trueblood Committee report in 1973, members of the financial community have urged research on such fundamental issues as the decision processes and information needs of financial statement users (Study Group 1973). Two fundamental questions have been formulated: Are financial reports useful to investors for their investment decisions? and What are the characteristics of the user group? Both these questions will be examined in depth in subsequent chapters. In this first chapter, we will trace the development of the search for user group objectives, with particular reference to the relationship between investors' behavior and the efficient market hypothesis.

The Objectives of Financial Reporting

In April 1971 the president of the American Institute of Certified Public Accountants (AICPA) appointed two committees to study the problems connected with establishing accounting principles. The Wheat Committee was to study the mechanisms for developing accounting principles. The Trueblood Committee's mandate was to define the objectives of financial statements. In June 1973, based on the recommendations of the Wheat Committee report published in March 1972, two new organizations—the Financial Accounting Foundation and the Financial Accounting Standards Board (FASB)—were established to replace the Accounting Principles Board (AICPA 1972). In October 1973, the Trueblood Committee report stated that the "broad objective of financial statements is to provide information useful for making economic decisions." This proposition has a respectable parentage. In 1961 George Staubus had written: "Where we recognize the investor group as a major consumer of the accountant's product, . . . we quickly arrive at the conclusion that a major objective of accounting is to provide quantitative economic information that will be useful in making economic decisions" (Staubus 1961:viii). The same proposition had been used by the American Accounting Association committee that prepared the AAA's "Statement of Basic Accounting Theory" (1966), in which accounting is defined as "the process of identifying, measuring, and communicating economic information to permit informed judgments and decisions by users of the information" (American Accounting Association 1966:1). The AICPA's Accounting Principles Board (APB) adopted this objective in its Statement 4: "The basic purpose of financial accounting and financial statements is to provide financial information about individual business enterprises that is useful in making economic decisions" (APB 1970:9). One of the largest CPA firms gave similar emphasis to the "decision usefulness" objective of accounting by stating that "general-purpose financial statements are designed to report to investors on the use of funds they have invested in their enterprise in such a way as to facilitate their investment decisions of the future" (Price Waterhouse & Co. 1971). Another AAA committee implies agreement: "To the extent that the accountant's notion of usefulness does *not* correspond to that of the user, financial reporting falls short of its stated objective, which is to serve the needs of the users" (AAA Subcommittee on Establishing Materiality 1976:244).

The FASB, which had inherited the task of setting objectives, published its tentative conclusions in December 1976. The study endorsed usefulness as the objective of accounting: "Financial statements of business enterprises should provide information, within the limits of financial accounting, that is useful to present and potential investors and creditors in making rational investment and credit decisions" (FASB 1974:3).

Finally, in its Statement of Financial Accounting Concepts (SFAC) 1 (November 1978), the FASB confirmed that "financial reporting should provide information that is useful to present and potential investors and creditors and other users in making rational investment, credit, and similar decisions" (FASB 1974:viii).

Investor Behavior and the Efficient Market

Even while various authorities have accepted the position that financial statements ought to be useful for investment decisions, other groups have been arguing that financial statements have not, in fact, been useful. Proponents of the efficient market hypothesis (EMH) postulate that information provided in corporate annual reports is not useful for making investment decisions. Apart from the weak form, which restricts the meaning of "information" to security price data only, the EMH asserts that annual report information will be impounded in the price of a security so rapidly that an investor cannot make abnormal (excess) returns in the market *on the basis of this information.*

Research aimed at providing empirical verification of the EMH is believed to tend toward its confirmation. In addition, research on the effects of accounting changes and other factors that affect financial reporting without necessarily affecting the economics of the reporting entity tends to show that investors are not "fooled" by such changes.

This type of research is characterized by massive statistical analyses of share price movements. By applying regression analysis on share prices across time, the researcher tries to determine which part of the movement of prices is due to changes affecting the market as a whole and which part is due to other identifiable factors. A regression equation is estimated with data from periods other than those which saw the publication of annual reports, in the form

$$R_{jt} = B_0 + B_1R_{mt} + u_{jt}$$

where

R_{jt} = relative price changes of share j in period t
R_{mt} = relative price changes for the market as a whole
u_{jt} = a residual, which should be equal to zero in periods other than those in which annual report information was published.

Using the estimated coefficients B_0 and B_1, one can calculate the residual price change for periods in which the financial statements were published. If the information affected investors' behaviors, the value u_{jt} during those periods would be other than zero.

Such research assumes that investors are using annual report information, even though they cannot profit from it. Indeed, models of investor behavior are usually incorporated explicitly, in the form of expected versus actual earnings per share and other variables.

George Benston, regarded by some as the father of this line of inquiry, wrote in 1974 that

> the value of reporting financial data for investors' decisions depends upon its usefulness and timeliness. The SEC's adherence to historically based "conservative" accounting procedures reduces the value of the data it requires be made public. Nevertheless, the question is an empirical one for which an empirical answer is sought. The studies that relate published accounting statement data with stock prices lead to the conclusion that the data either are not useful or have been fully impounded into stock prices before they are published. Since these studies use relatively simple decision models, evidence of the professional analysts' ability to use financial data for stock choices was reviewed. This evidence also sup-

> ports the conclusion that the accounting statements are not useful, or timely, or both. (Benston 1974:35)

Primary Users of Financial Statements

If the objective of financial statements is to provide useful information for making economic decisions, then the next question should be: "useful to whom?" Many groups use financial statements, principally present and potential investors, credit grantors, management, government agencies, and employees. Management has easy access to corporate information and can prescribe the form and content of financial statements for planning and control. Government agencies make decisions that affect the enterprise, but these users are "only indirectly affected by their decisions since they do not directly receive the benefits or incur the sacrifices" (Study Group 1973:18). The same argument may be applied to employees. The two major groups of financial statement users are therefore investors and creditors. This position was taken by the Accounting Principles Board: "Financial accounting presents general-purpose financial information that is designed to serve the common needs of owners, creditors, managers, and other users, with primary emphasis on the needs of present and potential owners and creditors" (APB Statement No. 4, APB 1970:47). According to the Study Group on the Objectives of Financial Statements, economic decisions for investors are similar to those of creditors. "While users may differ, their economic decisions are similar. Each user measures sacrifices and benefits in terms of the actual or prospective disbursement or receipt of cash. Further, the distinction between an investment and a credit decision often is not sharp" (Study Group 1973:18). According to a survey conducted by the Financial Executives Institute, approximately 90 percent of the companies surveyed reported that they gave first priority in financial reporting to existing shareholders, while no other user group was regarded as nearly so important (Rice 1973:11).

Investors' Decision Processes

For financial statements to be useful for investment decision making, they should cater to the information needs of investors. But what information do investors need, and what are their decision processes? As pointed out by the Study Group on the Objectives of Financial Statements, the accounting profession has no answers to these questions, as there has been essentially no research in this area (Study Group 1973:13).

Many accountants have stressed the importance of research on investors' decision processes and information needs. The AAA Subcommittee on Establishing Materiality Criteria wrote: "Given that agreement can be reached as to a particular user or user group on which attention should be focused, the next logical step in the establishment of materiality criteria is the determination of the information needs of such individuals. This, in turn, suggests the need of specifying their investment decision model(s)" (AAA Subcommittee on Establishing Materiality 1976:246–47).

There has been no agreement in the accounting profession as to which investor user group—individual investors, institutional investors, or financial analysts—should be the target user group for financial reporting. Perhaps it is assumed that they all have the same decision processes. One problem has been the lack of effective communication between any corporation and its stockholders. Early in 1964, Howard C. Greer, a university professor and corporate executive, indicated that corporations and public accountants did not provide useful information to the individual stockholder, "accounting's forgotten man" (Greer 1964:22–31). According to a more recent survey, 75 percent of corporate executives and "key publics" (i.e., professors of accounting, institutional investors and portfolio managers, stockbrokers and investment analysts, securities lawyers, certified public accountants, federal government officials, business editors and writers, and corporate social activists) did not believe that the individual investor had an equal opportunity for treatment in the market compared with large institutional investors (Arthur Andersen 1974:29). Also, according to a survey conducted in 1975 by Stockholders of America, Inc., only 32 percent of individual investors responding to a questionnaire expressed satisfaction with the information they received from corporations, while a year earlier a majority, or 61 percent, had reported satisfaction with corporate disclosure (Stockholders of America 1975:9).

For Whom Should Financial Statements Be Prepared?

The question of whether financial statements should be prepared primarily for the average layman or the knowledgeable reader has been discussed extensively. Some writers feel that accounting reports should use simpler language with little, if any, accounting jargon. A financial executive noted that the stockholder felt oppressed by the complexity of financial data and "frightened by what seems to him the incomprehensibility of accounting language. . . . He feels crushed, trampled down, and even burdened as by an abuse of power or authority" (Girdler 1963:71).

On the other hand, some writers point out that the financial statements are technical reports, that if these statements were deprived of their technical aspects they would no longer deliver their message effectively (see, for example, Littleton 1953). They argue that there is no reason to expect the uninformed layman to understand these reports without competent professional assistance just as he is not expected to comprehend a technical medical report or to decipher the legal jargon of a court opinion without professional assistance. These writers have argued that financial statements should be prepared primarily for professional analysts.

Over forty years ago, Paton and Littleton asserted that

> the day is past when accounting statements must be prepared for the man on the street who reads as he runs the last figures at the bottom of the income statements and no more. It is now necessary to produce statements which lend themselves to study by investment analysts; many more persons depend upon analysts' judgments, directly or indirectly, than follow their own untrained interpretations of corporations' reports. (Paton and Littleton 1940:101)

The list is rather long of writers who prefer professional financial analysts as the target user group. Some have gone so far as to argue that we can ignore the needs of individual investors, since they could not understand financial statements anyway. Buzby, for example, wrote that

> the line of reasoning used by Mautz and Sharaf in arriving at essentially the same conclusion provides additional support for this selection [of professional financial analysts as the target user group], which has excluded the average investor be he owner or creditor. This exclusion is justified on . . . the premise that most accounting information is not comprehensible to the average investor and cannot be made so without forgoing important elements of the accounting message. The best service that accounting can render the average investor is to provide more and better information to the professional analysts. (Buzby 1974:46)

The AAA Subcommittee on Establishing Materiality Criteria agreed with this viewpoint when they wrote that

> decisions made by many investors are probably derived from decisions and advice of sophisticated (professional) investors. Hence, concentration on the needs of professional investors indirectly helps meet the needs of the so-called average investors. (AAA Subcommittee on Establishing Materiality 1976:246)

The Study Group on the Objectives of Financial Statements, on the other hand, gave the following statement about its second objective:

> An objective of financial statements should serve primarily those users who have limited authority, ability, or resources to obtain information and who rely on financial statements as their principal source of information about an enterprise's economic activities. (Study Group 1973:17)

According to this view, financial statements should serve primarily not financial analysts on Wall Street but those investors who have no other means of obtaining information about the enterprise and require financial statements for their decisions.

An intermediate solution would be to prepare separate single-purpose financial statements to serve the information needs of different user groups. According to Mattessich, it is likely that "in the future several interrelated 'mono-purpose' accounting systems will replace one multipurpose establishment" (Mattessich 1964:9).

Research Objectives

The objective of the research reported here has been to provide answers to the following questions: Are financial statements used by investors to make their investment decisions? Are financial statements useful to investors for their investment decisions? Which investors have a reasonable understanding of business and economic activities and are willing to study the information with reasonable diligence?

To focus the issues more clearly, the following assumptions and hypotheses have been formulated:

Assumptions

a_1 = there exist periodic financial statements which are available to investors and their advisors and are intended to provide information for investment decisions.

a_2 = there exist three categories of financial statement users: individual investors, institutional investors, and financial analysts.

Hypotheses

h_1 = financial statements are used for investment decisions.

h_2 = financial statements are useful to investors and financial analysts for investment decisions.

h_3 = there are determinable differences between the importance of financial statements as viewed by each category of user as a source of information for investment decisions.

h_4 = institutional investors and financial analysts are homogeneous user groups.

h_5 = individual investors are not a homogeneous user group.

The Florida Survey: Research Design

The first stage of our research project consisted of a questionnaire survey of three user groups: individual investors, institutional investors, and financial analysts. This stage was called the Florida survey because the individual investors were selected randomly from the mailing list of a national stockbrokerage firm's Florida office. Institutional investors and financial analysts were randomly selected from various national directories.

After pretesting, 2,034 questionnaires were sent out, 1,034 to individual investors, and 500 each to institutional investors and financial analysts (see appendixes). This mailing took place in March 1976. One month later a second questionnaire was mailed to those who had not yet replied. A chi-square test was performed on all questions between the first and second batch of responses to test for bias between respondents and nonrespondents. This test disclosed no significant differences between the responses from the two mailings, so the two batches were merged and assumed to be representative of the populations surveyed.

The questionnaires were identical except that certain questions were adapted to the circumstances of each of the three groups. Part I of the questionnaire asked for respondents' investment objectives and views on the relative importance and usefulness of different sources of information presently available for making decisions about buying and holding or selling common stocks. It also questioned user needs for additional kinds of investment information not generally available at present. Part II asked respondents to disclose their personal characteristics, such as age, education, and investment experience.

Respondents were asked to answer questions in Part I using a 5-point scale (1 the lowest to 5 the highest importance). Similar surveys have been criticized for using this scale since the values of the points are not necessarily consistent between subjects: a rating of 3 may be interpreted as either "of moderate importance" or "fairly unimportant." Our own attention was directed primarily toward the unequivocal responses in the "1–2" and "4–5" categories. For purposes of computing means and in other statistical tests, however, all responses were used.

The National and International Surveys

To validate the research findings from the Florida survey, a national survey of United States individual investors was conducted in 1977, a few months after the Florida survey. To give the research study an international dimension, similar surveys of the three user groups—individual investors, institutional investors, and financial analysts—were conducted in the United Kingdom and New Zealand at the same time as the Florida survey.

A questionnaire identical to the ones used in the Florida survey was used in the national survey of individual investors. For investors in the United Kingdom and New Zealand, the questionnaires were modified slightly to accommodate the circumstances. (Modifications are noted on the questionnaires appended to this chapter.)

Data from the responses were transferred to computer cards and tabulated. A number of parametric and nonparametric statistical tests were performed by computer, using the same programs that had been used to analyze responses from the Florida survey: the chi-square test for nonresponse bias, frequency distributions, mean values, and T-tests between groups to identify significant differences and to attempt to relate importance of information to user characteristics. Additional tests that had not been used for the Florida survey were performed, specifically, the conservative F-test, a multiple range test (the Student-Newman-Keuls test), and the Goodman-Kruskal-Gamma measure of association. Factor analysis and multidiscriminant and multivariate analyses helped interpret the data.

1. *National survey of individual investors in the United States.* A mailing list of 2,000 shareholders was purchased from a professional mailing list company, who warranted it to be randomly selected from a list of investors in forty-nine states other than Florida.

Questionnaires were mailed to these individuals in January 1977, with a second mailing to those who failed to respond within six weeks. The two mailings produced 600 responses before the cutoff date, 554 of them usable, yielding a response rate of 27.7 percent of questionnaires mailed. Table 1.1 summarizes all responses, including those to the U.K. and N.Z. surveys described below. For U.S. and Florida individual investors, a chi-square test was performed on all questions between the first and second mailing responses. There being significant difference in answers to only five questions, responses from the two mailings were combined. Table 1.2 shows the chi-square values for the U.S. survey.

In the U.S. national surveys of institutional investors and financial analysts, responses were received from 165 institutional

Table 1.1
Analysis of responses to surveys

	Individual investors		Institutional investors		Financial analysts	
	Number of responses	Percentage of questionnaires returned	Number of responses	Percentage of questionnaires returned	Number of responses	Percentage of questionnaires returned
United States			165	34.5	123	33.3
Florida	182	21.5				
All other states	554	29.2				
United Kingdom	113	11.3	84	30.9	76	23.4
New Zealand	85	28.3	63	37.3	62	43.4

investors (34.5 percent) and 123 financial analysts (33.3 percent) (table 1.1).

2. *United Kingdom survey.* Simultaneously with the Florida survey, Professor Ali C. Osman of the Polytechnic of North London, England, conducted a parallel survey of the three user groups in the United Kingdom.

Individual investors were randomly selected from the share registers of three large public companies, a sugar refiner, a manufacturer of industrial gases, and a bank. Of the 1,000 questionnaires mailed to these shareholders, 113 (11.3 percent) were returned usable.

Questionnaires were also sent to 272 investment managers (institutional investors) and 325 investment analysts (financial analysts), selected in a manner similar to the selection of their U.S. counterparts. Responses were received from 84 of the former group and 76 of the latter, response rates of 30.88 percent and 23.38 percent respectively.

3. *New Zealand survey.* Also simultaneously with the Florida survey, Professor William Cotton of the University of Canterbury in New Zealand conducted an identical survey.

Questionnaires were sent to 300 individual investors randomly selected from the share registers of a New Zealand firm which keeps shareholder records for a number of public corporations in that country. Responses were obtained from 85 individual investors, yielding a response rate of 28.3 percent.

Questionnaires were also sent to 169 institutional investors, substantially all such investors in New Zealand, and to the entire known population of New Zealand financial analysts, who numbered 142. At the cutoff date, 63 responses were received from institutional investors and 62 from financial analysts, for response rates of 37.3 percent and 43.4 percent, respectively.

The responses from the four groups surveyed in the three countries are summarized in Table 1.1.

Table 1.2
Chi-square values of non-response bias test—
Individual investors
The United States survey

	Chi-square value	d.f.	Critical .05 value	Critical .01 value	Significant difference
I. Important objectives					
A. Dividend income	4.1159	4	9.49	13.28	No
B. Short-term capital gains	1.9063	4	9.49	13.28	No
C. Long-term capital gains	3.2724	4	9.49	13.28	No
D. Combination of dividend income & capital gains	.9211	4	9.49	13.28	No
II. Important sources of information					
A. Stockbroker's advice	2.8244	4	9.49	13.28	No
B. Advisory services	3.2397	4	9.49	13.28	No
C. Corporate annual reports	5.9826	4	9.49	13.28	No
D. Newspapers and magazines	11.6957	4	9.49*	13.28	Yes
E. Proxy statements	.9293	4	9.49	13.28	No
F. Advice of friends	1.1381	4	9.49	13.28	No
G. Tips and rumors	5.3879	4	9.49	13.28	No
III. Corporate report items					
A. President's letter					
Buying decision	8.5228	4	9.49	13.28	No
Holding or selling decision	1.6950	4	9.49	13.28	No
B. Pictorial material					
Buying decision	1.4607	4	9.49	13.28	No
Holding or selling decision	1.9392	4	9.49	13.28	No
C. Balance sheet					
Buying decision	7.0662	4	9.49	13.28	No
Holding or selling decision	11.2997	4	9.49*	13.28	Yes
D. Income statement					
Buying decision	12.2255	4	9.49*	13.28	Yes
Holding or selling decision	10.0485	4	9.49*	13.28	Yes
E. Statement of changes in financial position					
Buying decision	4.3324	4	9.49	13.28	No
Holding or selling decision	3.5581	4	9.49	13.28	No
F. Accounting policies					
Buying decision	3.4996	4	9.49	13.28	No
Holding or selling decision	5.1599	4	9.49	13.28	No
G. Other footnotes					
Buying decision	3.7508	4	9.49	13.28	No
Holding or selling decision	2.2796	4	9.49	13.28	No
H. Auditor's report					
Buying decision	3.2604	4	9.49	13.28	No
Holding or selling decision	6.2940	4	9.49	13.28	No
I. Summary of operations for the last 5–10 years					
Buying decision	9.1173	4	9.49	13.28	No
Holding or selling decision	10.1096	4	9.49*	13.28	Yes
J. Management's discussion and analysis of the summary of operations					
Buying decision	.5836	4	9.49	13.28	No
Holding or selling decision	2.6115	4	9.49	13.28	No

continued

Table 1.2 (continued)

	Chi-square value	d.f.	Critical .05 value	Critical .01 value	Significant difference
K. Sales and income by product line					
Buying decision	3.5235	4	9.49	13.28	No
Holding or selling decision	5.6898	4	9.49	13.28	No
L. Form 10-K report					
Buying decision	.4985	4	9.49	13.28	No
Holding or selling decision	1.4204	4	9.49	13.28	No
M. Are you aware that you can obtain a 10-K report from the company?	.0512	1	3.84	6.63	No
N. How many times have you requested a 10-K report in the last year?	4.7931	4	9.49	13.28	No
IV. Interim financial statements					
Buying decision	8.2224	4	9.49	13.28	No
Holding or selling decision	9.0568	4	9.49	13.28	No
V. How many trades based on information by interim financial statements	3.1175	3	7.81	11.34	No
VI. Forecast					
A. Sales revenue forecast for next year					
Buying decision	2.0645	4	9.49	13.28	No
Holding or selling decision	.9172	4	9.49	13.28	No
B. Cost of goods sold forecast for next year					
Buying decision	8.1432	4	9.49	13.28	No
Holding or selling decision	4.8236	4	9.49	13.28	No
C. Expenses forecast for next year					
Buying decision	3.9173	4	9.49	13.28	No
Holding or selling decision	5.6225	4	9.49	13.28	No
D. Earnings forecast for next year					
Buying decision	2.7738	4	9.49	13.28	No
Holding or selling decision	5.5804	4	9.49	13.28	No
E. Cash flow forecast for next year					
Buying decision	8.1471	4	9.49	13.28	No
Holding or selling decision	3.8112	4	9.49	13.28	No
F. Dividends forecast for next year					
Buying decision	4.1502	4	9.49	13.28	No
Holding or selling decision	2.7431	4	9.49	13.28	No
G. Additions to plant and equipment forecast for next year					
Buying decision	4.2443	4	9.49	13.28	No
Holding or selling decision	5.1183	4	9.49	13.28	No

:: Appendix 1

Questionnaire A

Information Needs of Financial Statement Users
Individual Investors

Our objective is to identify the importance which you place on each of the items listed in the questionnaire. For this purpose we are using a five-point scale, where 1 denotes the lowest and 5 denotes the highest importance. *Please circle the number 1 to 5 which reflects the importance of the item to you.*

PART I

I. When making decisions about buying, holding, or selling common stocks, what are your important objectives: *(Please circle one number for each item.)*

	Not Important			Very Important	
A. Dividend income	1	2	3	4	5
B. Profits from increase in market price within 6 months (short-term capital gains)	1	2	3	4	5
C. Profits from increase in market price after 6 months (long-term capital gains)	1	2	3	4	5
D. A combination of dividend income and capital gains	1	2	3	4	5
E. Other________________	1	2	3	4	5

Continued

The first stage of the research project, the Florida survey, consisted of a questionnaire survey of three user groups: individual investors, institutional investors, and financial analysts. After pretesting, in March 1976, 2,034 questionnaires were sent out, 1,034 to individual investors, and 500 each to institutional investors and financial analysts. The questionnaires are reproduced here.

To validate the research findings from the Florida survey, a national survey of the United States individual investors was conducted in 1977, a few months after the Florida survey. To give the research study an international dimension, similar surveys of the three user groups were conducted in the United Kingdom and New Zealand at the same time as the Florida survey. Modifications made to the questionnaires for the United Kingdom and New Zealand surveys are noted in the following questionnaires.

II. When making decisions about buying, holding, or selling common stocks, what are your important sources of information? (*Please circle one number for each item.*)

A. Stockbroker's advice	1	2	3	4	5
B. Advisory services	1	2	3	4	5
C. Corporate annual reports	1	2	3	4	5
D. Newspapers and magazines	1	2	3	4	5
E. Proxy statements	1	2	3	4	5
F. Advice of friends	1	2	3	4	5
G. Tips and rumors	1	2	3	4	5
H. Other____________________	1	2	3	4	5

III. In making decisions about buying, holding or selling common stocks, how do you rate the following parts of corporate published annual reports? (*Please circle one number for Buying Decision and one number for Holding or Selling Decision.*)

	Buying Decision					Holding or Selling Decision				
	Not Important			Very Important		Not Important			Very Important	
A. President's letter[1]	1	2	3	4	5	1	2	3	4	5
B. Pictorial material	1	2	3	4	5	1	2	3	4	5
C. Balance sheet	1	2	3	4	5	1	2	3	4	5
D. Income statement[2]	1	2	3	4	5	1	2	3	4	5
E. Statement of changes in financial position	1	2	3	4	5	1	2	3	4	5
F. Accounting policies	1	2	3	4	5	1	2	3	4	5
G. Other footnotes	1	2	3	4	5	1	2	3	4	5
H. Auditor's report	1	2	3	4	5	1	2	3	4	5
I. Summary of operations for the last 5 to 10 years	1	2	3	4	5	1	2	3	4	5
J. Management's discussion and analysis of the summary of operations	1	2	3	4	5	1	2	3	4	5
K. Sales and income by product line[3]	1	2	3	4	5	1	2	3	4	5
L. Form 10-K report [4]	1	2	3	4	5	1	2	3	4	5

M. Are you aware that a 10-K report can be obtained from the company on request?

Yes____ No____

N. If your answer to the previous question M was yes, how many times have you requested a 10-K report in the past year?

None___ Once___ Twice___ Three times___ More than three times____

IV. In making decisions about buying, holding or selling common stock, do you have the same degree of confidence in interim financial statements as in annual financial statements? (*Please circle one number for Buying Decision and one number for Holding or Selling Decision.*)

Buying Decision					Holding or Selling Decision				
Less Confidence		Same		More Confidence	Less Confidence		Same		More Confidence
1	2	3	4	5	1	2	3	4	5

[1]"Chairman's letter" for U.K. and N.Z. questionnaires.

[2]"Profit and loss account" for U.K. and N.Z. questionnaires.

[3]"Sales and profits by product line" for U.K. and N.Z. questionnaires.

[4]"Annual return filed with registrar of companies" for U.K. and N.Z. questionnaires.

Continued

V. How many trades (buy or sell) have you made in the past year based largely on information provided by interim financial statements? (*Please check one.*)
None___ 1 to 5___ 6 to 10___ 11 to 30___ Over 30___

VI. The subject matter in this section is not published in financial statements currently. In making decisions about buying, holding or selling common stock, how would you rate the usefulness of the following items if they were regularly published in financial statements? (*Please circle one number for Buying Decision and one number for Holding or Selling Decision.*)

	Buying Decision					Holding or Selling Decision				
	Not Useful			Very Useful		Not Useful			Very Useful	
A. Sales revenue forecast for next year	1	2	3	4	5	1	2	3	4	5
B. Cost of goods sold forecast for next year	1	2	3	4	5	1	2	3	4	5
C. Expenses forecast for next year	1	2	3	4	5	1	2	3	4	5
D. Earnings forecast for next year	1	2	3	4	5	1	2	3	4	5
E. Cash flow forecast for next year	1	2	3	4	5	1	2	3	4	5
F. Dividends forecast for next year	1	2	3	4	5	1	2	3	4	5
G. Additions to plant and equipment forecast for next year	1	2	3	4	5	1	2	3	4	5

PART II[1]

The following information will be very helpful for our study and will be kept confidential. However, if you wish, omit any item you choose not to answer.

I. What is the amount of your portfolio (common stock, preferred stock, and bonds and other securities) valued at cost? (*Please check one.*)
$1 - $999___ $1,000 - $9,999_____ $10,000 - $49,000_____
$50,000 - $99,999_____ $100,000 and over_____

II. What is the approximate amount of your common stock (valued at cost) in your portfolio? (*Please check one.*)
$0 - $999_____ $1,000 - $9,999_____ $10,000 - $49,000_____
$50,000 - $99,999_____ $100,000 and over_____

III. How long have you invested in common stock? (*Please check one.*)
Under 1 year_____ 1 - 4 years_____ 5 - 9 years_____
10 - 19 years_____ 20 years and over_____

IV. How many trades (buy and sale) of common stocks have you made in the past year? (*Please check one.*)
None_____ 1 - 9_____ 10 - 19_____
20 - 49_____ 50 and over_____

V. What is your annual income? (*Please check one.*)
Under $10,000_____ $10,000 - $19,999_____ $20,000 - $39,999_____
$40,000 - $79,999_____ $80,000 and over_____

[1] For United Kingdom similar categories were established in pound sterling.

Continued

Appendix 1. Questionnaire A: Individual Investors (continued)

VI. What level of education have you completed? *(Please check one.)*

Less than high school graduate_____
High school graduate_____
Some college_____ Major:______________________
College graduate_____ Major:______________________
Post graduate work_____ Major:______________________

VII. In what year were you born? __________
What is your current occupation?______________________

VIII. Have you had any formal educational training in accounting, finance or stock market investing?
No____ Yes____ (Describe briefly the nature of your training)__________
____
____

:: Appendix 2

Questionnaire B

Information Needs of Financial Statement Users
Institutional Investors

Our objective is to identify the importance which you place on each of the items listed in the questionnaire. For this purpose we are using a five-point scale, where 1 denotes the lowest and 5 denotes the highest importance. *Please circle the number 1 to 5 which reflects the importance of the item to you.*

PART I

I. When making decisions about buying, holding, or selling common stocks, what are your important objectives? (*Please circle one number for each item.*)

	Not Important				Very Important
A. Dividend income	1	2	3	4	5
B. Profits from increase in market price within 6 months (short-term capital gains)	1	2	3	4	5
C. Profits from increase in market price within 6 months (long-term capital gains)	1	2	3	4	5
D. A combination of dividend income and capital gains	1	2	3	4	5
E. Other __________	1	2	3	4	5

II. When making decisions about buying, holding, or selling common stocks, what are your important sources of information? (*Please circle one number for each item.*)

A. Stockbroker's advice	1	2	3	4	5
B. Advisory services	1	2	3	4	5
C. Corporate annual reports	1	2	3	4	5
D. Newspapers and magazines	1	2	3	4	5
E. Proxy statements	1	2	3	4	5
F. Advice of friends	1	2	3	4	5
G. Tips and rumors	1	2	3	4	5
H. Other __________	1	2	3	4	5

Continued

III. In making decisions about buying, holding or selling common stocks, how do you rate the following parts of corporate published annual reports? (*Please circle one number for Buying Decision and one number for Holding or Selling Decision.*)

	Buying Decision					Holding or Selling Decision				
	Not Important			Very Important		Not Important			Very Important	
A. President's letter [1]	1	2	3	4	5	1	2	3	4	5
B. Pictorial material	1	2	3	4	5	1	2	3	4	5
C. Balance sheet	1	2	3	4	5	1	2	3	4	5
D. Income statement[2]	1	2	3	4	5	1	2	3	4	5
E. Statements of changes in financial position	1	2	3	4	5	1	2	3	4	5
F. Accounting policies	1	2	3	4	5	1	2	3	4	5
G. Other footnotes	1	2	3	4	5	1	2	3	4	5
H. Auditor's report	1	2	3	4	5	1	2	3	4	5
I. Summary of operations for the last 5 to 10 years	1	2	3	4	5	1	2	3	4	5
J. Management's discussion and analysis of the summary of operations	1	2	3	4	5	1	2	3	4	5
K. Sales and income by product line [3]	1	2	3	4	5	1	2	3	4	5
L. Form 10-K report [4]	1	2	3	4	5	1	2	3	4	5

M. Are you aware that a 10-K report can be obtained from the company on request?

Yes ____ No ____

N. If your answer to the previous question M was yes, how many times have you requested a 10-K report in the past year?

None___ Once___ Twice___ Three times ___ More than three times ___

IV. In making decisions about buying, holding or selling common stocks, do you have the same degree of confidence in interim financial statements as in annual financial statements? (*Please circle one number for Buying Decision and one number for Holding or Selling Decision.*)

Buying Decision					Holding or Selling Decision				
Less Confidence		Same		More Confidence	Less Confidence		Same		More Confidence
1	2	3	4	5	1	2	3	4	5

V. How many trades (buy or sell) have you made in the past year based largely on information provided by interim financial statements? (*Please check one.*)

None___ 1 to 5___ 6 to 10___ 11 to 30___ Over 30___

[1] "Chairman's letter" for U.K. and N.Z. questionnaires.

[2] "Profit and loss account" for U.K. and N.Z. questionnaires.

[3] "Sales and profits by product line" for U.K. and N.Z. questionnaires.

[4] "Annual return filed with registrar of companies" for U.K. and N.Z. questionnaires.

Continued

VI. The subject matter in this section is not published in financial statements currently. In making decisions about buying, holding or selling common stock, how would you rate the usefulness of the following items if they were regularly published in financial statements? *(Please circle one number for Buying Decision and one number for Holding or Selling Decision.)*

	Buying Decision					Holding or Selling Decision				
	Not Useful			Very Useful		Not Useful				Very Useful
A. Sales revenue forecast for next year	1	2	3	4	5	1	2	3	4	5
B. Cost of goods sold forecast for next year	1	2	3	4	5	1	2	3	4	5
C. Expenses forecast for next year	1	2	3	4	5	1	2	3	4	5
D. Earnings forecast for next year	1	2	3	4	5	1	2	3	4	5
E. Cash flow forecast for next year	1	2	3	4	5	1	2	3	4	5
F. Dividends forecast for next year	1	2	3	4	5	1	2	3	4	5
G. Additions to plant and equipment forecast for next year	1	2	3	4	5	1	2	3	4	5

Part II[1]

I. What is the amount of portfolio that you are managing? *(Please check one.)*

$1 - $9,999___ $10,000 - $99,999___ $100,000 - $999,999___ $1,000,000 - $9,999,999___ $10,000,000 and over___

II. What is the approximate amount of common stock valued at cost in the portfolio that you are managing? *(Please check one.)*

$1 - $9,999___ $10,000 - $99,999___ $100,000 - $999,999___ $1,000,000 - $9,999,999___ $10,000,000 and over___

III. How many trades (buy or sale) have you made in the past year? *(Please check one.)*

None___ 1 - 9___ 10 - 19___ 20 - 49___ 50 and over___

IV. To the nearest year, how many years of experience do you have in your occupation?___

V. The title you are holding in your firm is______________________________

VI. Do you hold a university degree with a major in some field of business?
No___ Yes___ Name of school______________________________

VII. How many semester___quarter___hours of accounting did you complete successfully in your university education?______.

VIII. How many semester___quarter___hours of finance, investment analysis, financial analysis, or stock market investing did you complete successfully in your university education?__________.

[1] For United Kingdom similar categories were established in pound sterling.

:: Appendix 3

Questionnaire C

Information Needs of Financial Statement Users
Financial Analysts

Our objective is to identify the importance which you place on each of the items listed in the questionnaire. For this purpose we are using a five-point scale, where 1 denotes the lowest and 5 denotes the highest importance. *Please circle the number 1 to 5 which reflects the importance of the item to you.*

PART I

In making common stock investment recommendation, what are your important sources of information? (*Please circle one number for each item.*)

	Not Important				Very Important
A. Corporate annual reports	1	2	3	4	5
B. Corporate interim reports	1	2	3	4	5
C. Prospectuses	1	2	3	4	5
D. Newspapers and magazines	1	2	3	4	5
E. Corporate press releases	1	2	3	4	5
F. Communications with management	1	2	3	4	5
G. Advisory services	1	2	3	4	5
H. Proxy statements	1	2	3	4	5
I. Other ____________________					

In making common stock investment recommendations, how do you rate the following parts of corporate published annual reports? (*Please circle one number for Recommendation to Buy and one number for Recommendation to Hold or Sell.*)

	Recommendation to Buy					Recommendation to Hold or Sell				
	Not Important				Very Important	Not Important				Very Important
A. President's letter [1]	1	2	3	4	5	1	2	3	4	5
B. Pictorial material	1	2	3	4	5	1	2	3	4	5
C. Balance sheet	1	2	3	4	5	1	2	3	4	5

[1] "Chairman's letter" for U.K. and N.Z. questionnaires.

Continued

D. Income statement[1]	1	2	3	4	5	1	2	3	4	5
E. Statement of changes in financial position	1	2	3	4	5	1	2	3	4	5
F. Accounting policies	1	2	3	4	5	1	2	3	4	5
G. Other footnotes	1	2	3	4	5	1	2	3	4	5
H. Auditor's report	1	2	3	4	5	1	2	3	4	5
I. Summary of operations for the last 5 to 10 years	1	2	3	4	5	1	2	3	4	5
J. Management's discussion and analysis of the summary of operations	1	2	3	4	5	1	2	3	4	5
K. Sales and income by product line[2]	1	2	3	4	5	1	2	3	4	5
L. Form 10-K report[3]	1	2	3	4	5	1	2	3	4	5

M. Are you aware that a 10-K report can be obtained from the company on request?

Yes____ No____

N. If your answer to the previous question M was yes, how many times have you requested a 10-K report in the past year?

None____ Once____ Twice____ Three times____ More than three times____

III. In making common stock investment recommendations, do you have the same degree of confidence in interim financial statements as in annual financial statements? *(Please circle one number for Buying Decision and one number for Holding or Selling Decision)*

Buying Decision					Holding or Selling Decision				
Less Confidence		Same		More Confidence	Less Confidence		Same		More Confidence
1	2	3	4	5	1	2	3	4	5

IV. What percentage of your common stock investment recommendations made in the last years do you estimate was based largely on information provided by interim financial statements? *(Please check one.)*

None___ 1% - 5%___ 6% - 20%___ 21% - 50%___ Over 50%___

V. The subject matter in this section is not published in financial statements currently. In making common stock investment recommendations, how would you rate the usefulness of the following items if they were regularly published in financial statements? *(Please circle one number for Recommendation to Buy and one number for Recommendation to Hold or Sell.)*

	Recommendation to Buy					Recommendation to Hold or Sell				
	Not Useful				Very Useful	Not Useful				Very Useful
A. Sales revenue forecast for next year	1	2	3	4	5	1	2	3	4	5
B. Cost of goods sold forecast for next year	1	2	3	4	5	1	2	3	4	5
C. Expenses forecast for next year	1	2	3	4	5	1	2	3	4	5
D. Earnings forecast for next year	1	2	3	4	5	1	2	3	4	5
E. Cash flow forecast for next year	1	2	3	4	5	1	2	3	4	5
F. Dividends forecast for next year	1	2	3	4	5	1	2	3	4	5
G. Additions to plant and equipment forecast for next year	1	2	3	4	5	1	2	3	4	5

[1] "Profit and loss account" for U.K. and N.Z. questionnaires.

[2] "Sales and profits by product line" for U.K. and N.Z. questionnaires.

[3] "Annual return filed with registrar of companies" for U.K. and N.Z. questionnaires.

Continued

PART II [1]

I. Do you hold a university degree with a major in some field of business?
No___ Yes___ Name of school________________________________

II. How many semester___ quarter___hours of accounting did you complete successfully in your university education?________.

III. How many semester___ quarter___hours of finance, investment analysis, financial analysis, or stock market investing did you complete successfully in your university education?________.

IV. To the nearest year, how many years of experience do you have as a financial analyst and/or investment counselor?_______.

V. Would you characterize yourself primarily as a:

Security analyst?___ Fund or money manager?___ Investment counselor?___

Other?___ Describe____

____

____

[1] For United Kingdom similar categories were established in pound sterling.

2 :: Accounting and Investors: A Survey of the Literature

Our search of accounting literature yielded very few empirical studies on the uses of financial statements. Several empirical studies of financial analysts and individual investors have been conducted in recent years, but essentially no study has been made of how institutions use financial statements for equity investment decisions. This chapter reports previous research findings on the following questions: Are financial statements used for equity investment decisions? Are financial statements useful for equity investment decisions? What information is needed for equity investment decisions?

The Baker and Haslem Study (1973)

Individual common stock investors in metropolitan Washington, D.C., received questionnaires asking them to indicate the most important sources of information they used in evaluating common stocks. The results: 46.8 percent of the respondents rated stockbrokers as their most important source of information, while only 7.9 percent cited financial statements as their most important source (Baker and Haslem 1973:64–69).

Further, investors were instructed to indicate on a 5-point scale the relative importance of each of thirty-three items of information. Some items were currently reported in corporate annual reports, but most were not. The three most important items rated by the respondents were "future economic outlook of the company," "quality of management," and "future economic outlook of the industry in which the firm is a part" (pp. 66, 69).

The authors found that, although individual investors were primarily concerned with information relating to future expectations, they were also interested in historical facts. They concluded that "user information requirements for investment analysis may very well differ. Comparisons with other research findings suggest that individual investors may have different information needs than professional analysts" (p. 69).

The Epstein Study (1975)

Hoping to determine the usefulness of annual financial reports, Epstein found that only 15 percent of the respondents relied on annual reports as their primary basis for investment decisions while 48.8 percent of them relied on stockbrokers' advice (Epstein 1975:34).

Only 14.1 percent of the stockholders surveyed stated that corporate annual reports were very useful; 46.7 percent stated they were of moderate usefulness; 18.8 percent stated they were of little use; and 26.4 percent stated they were not useful at all (p. 42). Epstein concluded that corporate annual reports were not very useful to stockholders for investment decisions.

The Stockholders of America, Inc. Study (1975)

When this national nonprofit organization surveyed some 600 investors, its findings contradicted the two surveys cited above. To the question "How do you acquire information on a stock before investing?" 68 percent of the respondents indicated that they relied primarily on their own evaluation; 63 percent indicated that they also relied on a broker's advice (Stockholders of America 1975:2). Further, 85 percent of the respondents said that they "study the annual reports"; only 15 percent indicated that they did not (p. 11).

Regarding whether corporate annual reports were useful for equity investment decisions, the findings of this study were more equivocal. To the question "Do you feel that the information you presently receive from corporations is sufficient to keep you adequately informed of their progress and future plans?" 32 percent of the respondents answered in the affirmative, while 64 percent answered in the negative with respect to 1974 reports (p. 9).

The conclusion drawn was that corporations definitely needed to improve communications with their stockholders.

The Lee and Tweedie Study (United Kingdom, 1975)

These researchers sent questionnaires to individual shareholders of one of the largest industrial companies in the United Kingdom. The responses indicated that most respondents regarded annual financial reports as an important source of information for investment decisions. Financial press reports were considered the most important of all the other sources of information on companies. Stockbrokers' reports were read by many stockholders, but they were not considered as important a source as "occasional merger reports" or "half-yearly financial reports" (Lee and Tweedie, Autumn 1975:280–91).

Furthermore, of the 67.9 percent of respondents who said they understood the information contained in annual reports, 39.8 percent stated they found it relevant to their investment decisions while 28.1 percent found it irrelevant (Lee and Tweedie, Winter 1975:5). Using a 5-point scale (1 = maximum importance; 5 = no importance), "Profit and loss account" headed the list but with a mean of only 2.55; "Chairman's report" was second with a mean of 2.76 while "Auditor's report" was last, with a mean of 3.94 (Lee and Tweedie, Autumn 1975:283).

The question of whether stockholder information needs in the United Kingdom differ from those in the United States will be investigated later.

The Brenner Study (1970)

Stockholders, bankers, and financial analysts were asked for their views on the usefulness of current value information. The stockholder group showed a a majority neither for nor against "current value earnings per share" (CVEPS). On the average, 38 percent of stockholders seemed to be against CVEPS while 48 percent were in favor. On the other hand, 80 percent of the financial analysts disagreed or strongly disagreed with CVEPS; only 12 percent favored them (Brenner 1970:161).

Brenner concluded that different user groups had different information needs.

The Briggs Study (United Kingdom, 1975)

Some studies have investigated banking institutions' use of financial statements for credit-granting decisions (for instance, Brenner 1970; Estes 1968). But a search of accounting literature has failed to discover any empirical studies on institutional investors' use of financial reports for equity investment decisions. The Briggs study conducted in the United Kingdom was exploratory in nature. Briggs interviewed twenty-five stockbrokers and officials of unit or investment trusts, including some merchant banks that have their own trusts. To the question "How useful is the information found in published corporate reports?" there was almost unanimous agreement that accounting reports were essential. But the majority of those interviewed also claimed that they tried to modify some items in the report (Briggs 1975:19).

This study also attempted to elicit views on what information should be provided in annual reports. The conclusions: "There was a preference for replacement cost (about two-thirds), although about half expressed interest as well in a measure of realizable value, but sometimes with the reservation that the latter approach should be applied only if liquidation were expected" (pp. 19–20)

Briggs's report must be seen as a subjective review of opinions expressed during interviews. In addition, the opinions of trust managers were not distinguished from those of financial analysts.

The Mautz Study (1968)

In trying to identify the information needs of financial analysts in respect to financial reporting by diversified companies,

Mautz asked financial analysts to rate the relative importance of several sources of information in their analysis of operating results by segments of conglomerate companies. Financial analysts gave financial statements 67 percentage points for their relative importance while the next most important source, interviews with management, received 14 points (Mautz 1968:301).

The Financial Analysts Federation Study (1972)

As a step toward producing its position paper for the study group on the Objectives of Financial Statements, the Financial Analysts Federation conducted an interview survey among its senior members on several topics such as the objectives of accounting statements, accounting principles, the quality of accounting, and accounting in the investment process (Financial Analysts Federation 1972). On the question of the sources of information for their investment decisions or recommendations, most financial analysts commented that accounting information was vital for their analyses of different companies (pp. A-6–A-9).

The Pankoff and Virgil Study (1970)

In this "laboratory experiment," thirty-two analysts from St. Louis and New York City were asked to make investment decisions by using hypothetical net worth to purchase price ratio information. The authors concluded that they had not found much empirical support for the belief that accounting information was generally and highly useful for decision making, although the analysts wanted certain kinds of accounting information badly enough to pay for them (Pankoff and Virgil 1970:23).

The Chandra Study (1974)

Certified public accountants and financial analysts were requested to rate the importance of fifty-eight items of information for equity investment decisions. Conclusion: accountants generally did not value information for equity investment decisions in the same manner as financial analysts (Chandra 1974:733–42).

The Securities and Exchange Commission (SEC) Study (1976–77)

The SEC used a questionnaire to survey eleven thousand individual U.S. investors as part of the investigations of the Advisory Committee on Corporate Disclosure. These investors each owned fewer than 1,000 shares of stock in fifteen publicly held corporations. Table 8 of the Committee's Report, "Value Ranking of Information Types—All Investors," revealed that 50 percent of the respondents rated financial statements "extremely useful," 36 percent rated them "moderately useful," and only

3 percent rated them "not at all useful" (*Report of the Advisory Committee* 1977).

The Bradish Study (1965)

From time to time, writers have discussed the information needs of professional financial analysts (e.g., Anderson 1967; Carlson 1974; Norr 1970; Backer 1966; Tevelow 1971). But empirical studies of their information needs are not as numerous. Bradish interviewed financial analysts to elicit their views on the disclosure of a number of troublesome items, such as long-term leases and funds-flow statements (Bradish 1965:757–66).

The Estes Study (1968)

Financial analysts, bank loan and credit officers, and financial executives were surveyed to elicit their views on the usefulness of current cost information and price-level adjusted information (Estes 1968).

The Rao Study (1974)

This survey analyzed the accounting information needs of three selected groups of users: investment advisors, financial analysts, and scholars of accounting. Rao reported that these user groups noted many information deficiencies in the annual report (Rao 1975).

The Duff and Phelps Report (1975)

The public accounting firm of Arthur Andersen & Co. engaged a firm of financial analysts, Duff and Phelps, Inc., to examine corporate annual reporting. Their report stated as a fundamental assumption that "shareholder reports are the basic channel of communication with all investors" (Duff and Phelps 1966:ix).

This brief survey of previous research on investors' uses of financial statements demonstrates clearly the controversial aspect of the subject. Some researchers purport to find that investors place great importance on financial statement information for their investment decisions. Others place a low value on the importance of this information source. We thus decided to approach a resolution of this apparent conflict by attempting ourselves to identify investors' investment objectives before ascertaining the relative importance of different information sources.

3 :: Investors' Investment Objectives

Investors' investment objectives will influence their choice of information sources. An analogy can be made with persons who are interested in the cinema. If their objective is to familiarize themselves with the current state of the cinematic art, the preferred information source will be the specialized journals and cultural magazines that contain lengthy film reviews and critical articles. If their objective is to go out to a movie, the preferred information source will be the daily newspaper.

Question I of the questionnaires mailed to individual and institutional investors in all three test countries asked, "When making decisions about buying, holding, or selling common stocks, what are your important objectives?" (Financial analysts were not asked this question.)

Tables 3.1 and 3.2 show that for both investor groups in all three countries the most important investment objective was long-term income and capital gains.

For U.S. investors, the most important objective was long-term capital gains; for U.K. and N.Z. investors, it was a combination of dividend income and long-term capital gains. This difference should elicit no surprise, since at the time the questionnaire was being completed dividend yields were substantially higher in the United Kingdom than in the United States. The different tax systems may also be a factor. That the N.Z. responses were identical in rankings and relative weights to the U.K. responses lends weight to this last supposition, because the two countries have similar income tax laws.

We compared the findings for U.S. individual investors with those for Florida investors. Short-term capital gain was the only objective for which responses were statistically different; Florida investors rated short-term capital gains more important than did U.S. investors. Other than that, the rankings of the four objectives and the ratings of all objectives other than short-term capital gains were virtually the same for the U.S. and Florida samples.

Both investor groups in all three countries rated dividend income third and short-term capital gains fourth. The responses of individual investors in the three countries showed that the objective of short-term capital gains was rated more important by investors in the United States and New Zealand than by those in the United Kingdom. Long-term capital gains, however, were

Table 3.1
Mean values and T-test results—Importance of individual investors' investment objectives

	$\bar{X}$			T (Probability)		
Investment objectives	U.S.	U.K.	N.Z.	U.S. : U.K.	U.S. : N.Z.	U.K. : N.Z.
Dividend income	3.350	3.219	3.374	−.90 (.368)	−.19 (.848)	−.85 (.395)
Short-term capital gains	2.202	1.780	2.253	−3.15 (.002)**	−.34 (.736)	−.242 (.017)*
Long-term capital gains	4.154	3.895	4.062	−1.99 (.049)*	−.71 (.482)	−.97 (.333)
Combination of dividend income and capital gains	4.091	3.952	4.132	−1.18 (.239)	−.30 (.764)	−1.12 (.265)

*Significant at level of 0.05
**Significant at levels of 0.05 and 0.01

Table 3.2
Mean values and T-test results—importance of institutional investors' investment objectives

	$\bar{X}$			T (Probability)		
Investment objectives	U.S.	U.K.	N.Z.	U.S. : U.K.	U.S. : N.Z.	U.K. : N.Z.
Dividend income	3.243	3.702	3.603	2.53 (.013)*	.48 (.634)	2.33 (.022)*
Short-term capital gains	2.376	2.609	2.085	1.11 (.271)	2.17 (.033)*	−1.58 (.117)
Long-term capital gains	4.232	3.952	4.017	−1.91 (.059)	− .36 (.719)	−1.43 (.156)
Combination of dividend income and capital gains	4.097	4.212	4.433	.76 (.447)	−1.35 (.178)	2.49 (.014)*

*Significant at level of 0.05

rated slightly more important by U.S. and N.Z. investors than by investors in the United Kingdom.

Institutional investors also rated dividend income third and short-term capital gains fourth; investors in New Zealand, however, placed relatively low importance on short-term capital gains.

Tables 3.1 and 3.2 also show the results of T-tests performed to compare these six groups. Individual investors produced three statistically significant differences: in the United States, they placed more importance on both dividend income and short-term capital gains than they did in the United Kingdom, and in New Zealand they placed more importance on short-term capital gains than they did in the United Kingdom. Institutional investors produced four significant differences: in the United Kingdom, they placed more importance on dividend income than they did in the United States and New Zealand; U.S. investors placed more importance on short-term capital gains than did investors in New Zealand; and N.Z. investors placed more importance on a combination of dividend income and capital gains than did those in the United Kingdom.

We find these results noteworthy. Even though the stock markets in these three countries may reflect the activities of large numbers of traders, the bulk of the stocks quoted on those markets appear to be held by investors for long intervals. This finding must be relevant to researchers who attempt to test the efficient market hypothesis by analyzing weekly, monthly, or other short-period price movements of common stocks.

The most important investment objective for both individual and institutional investors is thus determined to be either long-term capital gains or a combination of dividend income and capital gains. These objectives are considerably more important than short-term capital gains. It would appear that prediction of short-term cash flows would not be one of the more important investor uses of financial statements, and long-term projections of cash flows are particularly speculative.

The long-term nature of investment objectives is, of course, important in evaluating investors' information sources. If investors' objectives were short term in nature, one would expect the most important information sources to be daily newspapers and stockbrokers' advice. As we shall see, the respondents' importance ratings of the information sources listed in the questionnaires were consistent with their long-term objectives.

4 :: Investment information sources

The questionnaire appended to chapter 1 included groups of questions on investment objectives, information sources, and personal characteristics of the respondents. We turn in chapters 4 and 5 to the task of identifying and evaluating information sources.

The three groups of respondents in the United States, the United Kingdom, and New Zealand were asked to rate the importance of various sources of information for equity investment decisions. Specifically, they were asked, "When making decisions about buying, holding, or selling common stocks, what are your important sources of information?" Investors, both individuals and those investing for institutions, specified sources of information slightly different from those named by financial analysts (table 4.1). The questionnaires included four questions common to all three groups plus three additional questions for investors and four additional questions for financial analysts.

Individual Investors

Mean values and T-test results of the responses from individual investors in the three countries appear in table 4.2. "Corporate annual reports" was considered the most important source of information by U.S. investors as indicated by the mean value; in addition, 45.7 percent rated this source 4 or 5. (Remember, an answer of 5 on this question meant "greatest importance.") "Newspapers and magazines" came second and was rated 4 or 5 by 37.1 percent. "Advisory services" ranked third in importance, slightly above "stockbroker's advice." "Proxy statements" ranked fifth in importance, while the other two information sources, "advice of friends" and "tips and rumors," were considered of minor importance.

Table 4.3 shows the results of the Student-Newman-Keuls (S-N-K) multiple range test, which confirmed that the importance given by this group of respondents to corporate annual reports was significantly higher statistically than any of the other sources rated.

The responses of U.S. individual investors were compared with those of Florida investors. The rankings of the information sources by these two groups were almost identical, except that U.S. individual investors ranked advisory services slightly above

Table 4.1
Information sources

Individual investors and institutional investors	Financial analysts
Stockbroker's advice	Corporate annual reports
Advisory service	Corporate interim reports[b]
Corporate annual reports	Prospectuses
Newspapers and magazines	Newspapers and magazines
Proxy statements[a]	Corporate press releases
Advice of friends	Communications with management
Tips and rumors	Advisory services
	Proxy statements

[a]"Published Statements by Company Directors" for U.K. and N.Z. questionnaires.
[b]"Company Half-Yearly Reports" for U.K. and N.Z. questionnaires.

Table 4.2
Mean values and T-test results—importance of individual investors' information sources

	$\bar{X}$			T (Probability)		
Information sources	U.S.	U.K.	N.Z.	U.S. : U.K.	U.S. : N.Z.	U.K. : N.Z.
Stockbroker's advice	2.88	3.165	3.374	1.82 (.071)	−3.02 (.003)**	− .98 (.328)
Advisory services	2.99	2.022	2.026	−6.22 (.000)**	6.53 (.000)**	− .02 (.985)
Corporate annual reports	3.24	2.733	3.222	−3.53 (.001)**	.13 (.898)	−2.61 (.010)**
Newspapers and magazines	3.07	3.324	3.468	2.00 (.047)*	−2.61 (.011)*	− .78 (.434)
Proxy statements	2.31	2.296	2.650	− .11 (.910)	−2.23 (.028)*	−1.91 (.058)
Advice of friends	1.85	1.910	1.812	.50 (.620)	.25 (.802)	.56 (.576)
Tips and rumors	1.40	1.642	1.469	2.00 (.048)*	− .74 (.464)	1.15 (.251)

*Significant at level of 0.05
**Significant at levels of 0.05 and 0.01

stockbroker's advice, while Florida investors reversed the importance of the two categories. A T-test comparing the responses of these two groups showed that these differences were not statistically significant values. U.S. investors rated only "advice of friends" and "tips and rumors" significantly less important than Florida investors.

Both U.K. and N.Z. individual investors rated "newspapers and magazines" their most important source of information, with mean values of 3.32 and 3.47 respectively. In fact, U.K. and N.Z. individual investors ranked the seven information sources in almost identical order. They rated "sharebroker's advice" second, "corporate annual reports" third, and "published statements of company directors" ("proxy statements" in the U.S. survey) fourth and ahead of "advisory services." Like their counterparts in the United States, U.K. and N.Z. individual investors rated "advice of friends" and "tips and rumors" as relatively unimportant.

The T-test results show that corporate annual reports are significantly more important to investors in the United States than in the United Kingdom; stockbroker's advice is more important in New Zealand than in the United States; and advisory services are more important in the United States than in either of the other countries.

While we have not investigated the reasons for these differences, they may lie in qualitative differences between the information sources themselves in the three countries. Corporate reporting by U.S. companies may be more informative. The financial press in the United Kingdom and New Zealand may be more analytical than its U.S. counterpart and therefore may perform for investors in those countries some of the services that U.S. investors must perform for themselves. Again, stockbrokers in the United Kingdom and New Zealand are not permitted to deal for their own accounts and are restricted to functioning as agents. This fact would explain why investors in those countries have considerable confidence in brokers' recommendations and rely upon them as a source of advice. This aspect of our subject of study—the variable nature of the information sources—appears to merit more research.

Table 4.3
Student-Newman-Keuls multiple range test for information sources
Individual investors
The United States survey

Sources of information (See key below.)	Mean differences						Multiple ranges α = .05	Multiple ranges α = .01
A↘ ↙G	1.8034**						.2159	.2548
B↘ ↙F	1.6517**	1.3483**					.2085	.2480
C↘ ↙E	1.5406**	1.1966**	.8846**				.1994	.2397
D↘ ↙D	1.4509**	1.0855**	.7329**	.3525**			.1876	.2290
E↘ ↙C	.9188**	.9958**	.6218**	.2008*	.2628**		.1709	.2138
F↘ ↙B	.4551**	.4637**	.5321**	.0897	.1111	.1517*	.1426	.1885

*Significant at .05 level.
**Significant at .01 level.

Key to Corporate Annual Report Items		Mean Value	Key to Corporate Annual Report Items		Mean Value
A	Corporate annual reports	3.1816	E	Proxy statements	2.2970
			F	Advice of friends	1.8333
[B	Newspapers and magazines	3.0299	G	Tips and rumors	1.3782
[C	Advisory services	2.9188			
D	Stockbroker's advice	2.8291			

[= Difference between mean values not significant.

Table 4.4
Mean values and T-test results—importance of institutional investors' information sources

Information sources	$\bar{X}$ U.S.	U.K.	N.Z.	T (Probability) U.S. : U.K.	U.K. : N.Z.	U.S. : N.Z.
Stockbroker's advice	2.516	3.872	3.450	7.66 (.000)**	2.11 (.038)*	5.60 (.000)**
Advisory services	3.082	2.646	3.052	−2.39 (.018)*	−1.84 (.068)	− .16 (.871)
Corporate annual reports	3.440	3.952	3.377	3.53 (.001)**	3.00 (.003)**	− .36 (.723)
Newspapers and magazines	2.617	2.905	2.950	1.98 (.050)*	− .24 (.811)	2.04 (.044)*
Proxy statements	2.360	3.169	3.000	5.19 (.000)**	.84 (.403)	3.38 (.001)**
Advice of friends	1.397	1.370	1.550	− .21 (.833)	−1.08 (.282)	1.10 (.274)
Tips and rumors	1.353	1.333	1.414	− .17 (.869)	− .60 (.548)	.49 (.628)

*Significant at level of 0.05
**Significant at levels of 0.05 and 0.01

Institutional Investors

Mean values and T-test results of the responses of institutional investors are tabulated for the three countries in table 4.4. U.S. and U.K. respondents rated corporate annual reports their most important source of information; 47.8 percent of U.S. respondents and 71.4 percent of U.K. respondents gave this source a 4 or 5. Institutional investors in New Zealand rated this source slightly lower than stockbroker's advice; 47.6 percent gave corporate annual reports a 4 or 5 compared with 48.4 percent for stockbroker's advice. In all cases, advisory services were rated lower than annual reports, but U.S. respondents rated them second. Newspapers and magazines were rated third and stockbroker's advice fourth. Advice of friends and tips and rumors were again relatively unimportant.

The S-N-K multiple range test of the information sources of institutional investors in the United States confirmed that the importance given to corporate annual reports was significantly higher than that given to any of the other sources (table 4.5).

Responses of institutional investors in the United Kingdom and New Zealand did show a somewhat different pattern. Institutional investors in the United Kingdom rated stockbroker's advice second after company annual reports, published statements by company directors third, and newspapers and magazines fourth. Advice of friends and tips and rumors were again rated unimportant.

Institutional investors in New Zealand, on the other hand, rated stockbroker's advice first, with company annual reports a very close second. Advisory services were rated third and published statements by company directors fourth. Advice of friends and tips and rumors were again rated unimportant.

As there were a number of intercountry differences on the importance of institutional investors' information sources, table 4.6 lists them. It was derived from the T-test results in table 4.4.

Table 4.5
Student-Newman-Keuls multiple range test for information sources
Institutional investors
The United States survey

Sources of information (See key below.) — Mean differences

Mean differences						Multiple ranges α=.05	Multiple ranges α=.01
A–G 2.1528**						.3508	.4140
B–G 1.8264**	A–F 1.9930**					.3388	.4030
C–G 1.3612**	B–F 1.6666**	A–E 1.0625**				.3240	.3895
D–G 1.2362**	C–F 1.2014**	B–E .7361**	A–D .9166**			.3048	.3720
E–G 1.0903**	D–F 1.0764**	C–E .2709	B–D .5902**	A–C .7916**		.2776	.3474
F–G .1598	E–F .9305**	D–E .1459	C–D .1250	B–C .4652**	A–B .3264**	.2316	.3062

*Significant at .05 level.
**Significant at .01 level.

Key to Corporate Annual Report Items		Mean Value
A	Corporate annual reports	3.4097
B	Advisory services	3.0833
[C	Newspapers and magazines	2.6181
[D	Stockbroker's advice	2.4931
[E	Proxy statements	2.3472
[F	Advice of friends	1.4167
[G	Tips and rumors	1.2569

[= Difference between mean values not significant.

Table 4.6
Intercountry comparison of importance
of institutional investors' information sources

U.S. : U.K.	More important
Stockbroker's advice	U.K.
Advisory services	U.S.
Corporate annual reports	U.K.
Newspapers and magazines	U.K.
Proxy statements	U.K.
U.S. : N.Z.	**More important**
Stockbroker's advice	N.Z.
Newspapers and magazines	N.Z.
Proxy statements	N.Z.
U.K. : N.Z.	**More important**
Stockbroker's advice	U.K.
Corporate annual reports	U.K.

Table 4.7
Mean values and T-test results—importance of financial analysts' information sources

Information sources	$\bar{X}$ U.S.	U.K.	N.Z.	T (Probability) U.S. : U.K.	U.S. : N.Z.	U.K. : N.Z.
Corporate interim reports	3.868	3.973	4.000	.69 (.491)	.80 (.425)	− .16 (.876)
Advisory services	2.934	2.342	2.927	−3.33 (.001)**	− .03 (.975)	−2.53 (.013)*
Corporate annual reports	4.355	4.608	4.508	1.98 (.049)*	1.13 (.258)	.76 (.449)
Newspapers and magazines	2.883	3.054	3.138	1.18 (.240)	1.65 (.103)	− .48 (.631)
Proxy statements	2.890	2.873	3.583	− .10 (.924)	3.65 (.000)**	−3.75 (.000)**
Corporate press releases	2.897	2.892	3.759	− .03 (.973)	5.01 (.000)**	−4.76 (.000)**
Communications with management	4.117	4.622	3.883	3.66 (.000)**	−1.23 (.219)	4.13 (.000)**
Prospectuses	4.239	3.986	3.593	−1.52 (.130)	−3.27 (.001)**	1.84 (.069)

*Significant at levels of 0.05
**Significant at levels of 0.05 and 0.01

Financial Analysts

Mean values and T-test results of the responses of financial analysts in the three countries are tabulated in table 4.7. All three groups of financial analysts rated corporate annual reports as even more important sources of information than did individual and institutional investors; 82.6 percent of U.S. financial analysts gave this source a rank of 4 or 5. U.S. analysts rated annual reports first and prospectuses second, communications with management third, and interim reports fourth. In contrast, corporate press releases had a rank mean value of only 2.9, suggesting that financial analysts rate information originating from accountants as more important than information originating from public relations specialists.

Table 4.8 displays the results of the S-N-K multiple range test performed on the importance placed on information sources by U.S. financial analysts. They indicate that the differences between analysts' three most important sources—corporate annual reports, prospectuses, and communications with management—were not statistically significant. But the differences between the importance of these three sources and that of any of the remaining five sources were statistically different.

Financial analysts in the United Kingdom rated communications with management their most important source of information, with 91.7 percent of them rating this source 4 or 5. Company annual reports were rated a very close second, 90.4 percent of the respondents rating this source 4 or 5. Prospectuses were rated third and company half-yearly reports fourth. Then follow newspapers and magazines, company press releases, and published statements by company directors (rated less important with a mean of 2.92 and 2.9 respectively), and finally advisory services.

Table 4.8
Student-Newman-Keuls multiple range test for information sources
Financial analysts
The United States survey

Sources of information (See key below.) — Mean differences — Multiple ranges

	Mean differences								Multiple ranges α = .05	Multiple ranges α = .01
A↘	1.5000**							↙H	.4132	.4858
B↘	1.4057**	1.4811**						↙G	.4016	.4750
C↘	1.3019**	1.3868**	1.4717**					↙F	.3878	.4622
D↘	.9717**	1.2830**	1.3774**	1.4340**				↙E	.3708	.4466
E↘	.0660	.9528**	1.2736**	1.3397**	.5283**			↙D	.3487	.4263
F↘	.0283	.0471	.9434**	1.2359**	.4340**	.1981		↙C	.3174	.3979
G↘	.0189	.0094	.0377	.9057**	.3302*	.1038	.0943	↙B	.2647	.3505

*Significant at .05 level.
**Significant at .01 level.

Key to Corporate Annual Report Items	Mean Value	Key to Corporate Annual Report Items	Mean Value
⌈A Corporate annual reports	4.3585	⌈E Advisory services	2.9245
B Prospectuses	4.2642	F Proxy statements	2.8868
⌊C Communications with management	4.1604	G Newspapers and magazines	2.8774
		⌊H Corporate press releases	2.8585
D Corporate interim reports	3.8302		

[= Difference between mean values not significant.

Financial analysts in New Zealand rated company annual reports their most important source of information, 86.9 percent of these respondents rating this source 4 or 5. Company half-yearly reports were second, rated 4 or 5 by 68.9 percent. Communications with management were third, rated 4 or 5 by 66.9 percent. Company press releases were rated more important by New Zealand financial analysts than by their counterparts in the United States and the United Kingdom.

Table 4.9 summarizes the intercountry differences on the importance of financial analysts' information sources, again based on the results of the T-tests.

Conclusion

For convenience, the mean values given to the information sources by the three groups in the three countries are shown in table 4.10. These mean values are converted into order rankings in table 4.11. The similarities and differences commented on above are clearly apparent. It is noteworthy that corporate annual reports rank in first place five times, in second place twice,

Table 4.9
Intercountry comparison of importance of financial analysts' information sources

U.S. : U.K.	More important
Advisory services	U.S.
Corporate annual reports	U.K.
Communications with management	U.K.
U.S. : N.Z.	**More important**
Proxy statements	N.Z.
Corporate press releases	N.Z.
Prospectuses	U.S.
U.K. : N.Z.	**More important**
Advisory services	N.Z.
Proxy statements	N.Z.
Corporate press releases	N.Z.
Communications with management	U.K.

Table 4.10
Mean values of importance of investor and financial analysts' sources of investment information

	Individual investors			Institutional investors			Financial analysts		
Information sources	U.S.	U.K.	N.Z.	U.S.	U.K.	N.Z.	U.S.	U.K.	N.Z.
Stockbroker's advice	2.88	3.17	3.37	2.52	3.87	3.45	—	—	—
Advisory service	2.99	2.02	2.03	3.08	2.65	3.05	2.93	2.31	2.93
Corporate annual reports	3.24	2.73	3.22	3.44	3.95	3.38	4.36	4.60	4.51
Newspapers and magazines	3.07	3.32	3.47	2.62	2.91	2.95	2.88	3.03	3.14
Proxy statements[b]	2.31	2.30	2.65	2.36	3.17	3.00	2.89	2.90	3.58
Advice of friends	1.85	1.19	1.81	1.40	1.37	1.55	—	—	—
Tips and rumors	1.60	1.64	1.47	1.35	1.33	1.41	—	—	—
Prospectuses[a]							4.24	4.03	3.59
Communications with management[a]							4.12	4.64	3.88
Corporate interim reports[a, c]							3.87	3.99	4.00
Corporate press releases[a]							2.90	2.92	3.76

[a]Financial analysts only.
[b]"Published Statement by Company Directors" for questionnaires used in U.K. and N.Z.
[c]"Company Half-Yearly Reports" for questionnaires used in U.K. and N.Z.

and in third place twice. The low rankings of proxy statements is surprising and appears to merit further investigation.

The principal observation we made is that financial analysts as a whole placed greater importance on corporate annual reports than did institutional investors; institutional investors, in turn, placed greater importance on such reports than did individual investors. Inasmuch as securities analysis is central to the

Table 4.11

Intercountry ranking of information sources in order of relative importance

	United States			United Kingdom			New Zealand		
	Individual investors	Institutional investors	Financial analysts	Individual investors	Institutional investors	Financial analysts	Individual investors	Institutional investors	Financial analysts
Corporate annual reports	1	1	1	3	1	2	3	2	1
Newspapers and magazines	2	3	8	1	2	5	1	5	7
Advisory services	3	2	5	5	5	8	5	3	8
Stockbroker's advice	4	4	—	2	3	—	2	1	—
Proxy statements[b]	5	5	7	4	4	7	4	4	6
Advice of friends	6	6	—	6	6	—	6	6	—
Tips and rumors	7	7	—	7	7	—	7	7	—
Prospectuses[a]	—	—	2	—	—	3	—	—	5
Communications with management[a]	—	—	3	—	—	1	—	—	3
Interim reports[a, c]	—	—	4	—	—	4	—	—	2
Press releases[a]	—	—	6	—	—	6	—	—	4

[a]Financial analysts only.

[b]"Published Statement by Company Directors" for questionnaires used in U.K. and N.Z.

[c]"Company Half-Yearly Reports" for quesionnaires used in U.K. and N.Z.

responsibilities of institutional investors and financial analysts, and since both user groups are conventionally classified as "sophisticated," we are clearly justified in inferring that corporate annual reports represent information useful for investment decisions.

5 :: Investors' Views on the Importance of Corporate Annual Report Items

Having established that investors and financial analysts use corporate annual reports, we can now address an important question for the accounting profession: "Are financial statements as they are now prepared useful for investment decisions?"

To answer this question, we presented users with a list of items selected from corporate annual reports, asking them to evaluate the importance of each item in their decisions regarding buying and holding or selling common stocks. The three user groups in the three countries were asked to rate the importance of these selected elements for these decisions.

Respondents were given the opportunity to rate the importance of these components for "buying decisions" separately from "holding or selling decisions." The elements of the corporate annual report listed were these:

President's letter (chairman's letter for U.K. and N.Z. questionnaires)
Pictorial material
Balance sheet
Income statement (profit and loss account for U.K. and N.Z. questionnaires)
Statement of changes in financial position
Accounting policies
Other footnotes
Auditor's report
Summary of operations for the last five to ten years
Management's discussion and analysis of the summary of operations
Sales and income by product line (sales and profits by product line for U.K. and N.Z. questionnaires)

In addition, the annual financial Form 10-K report (annual return filed with registrar of companies in U.K. and N.Z. questionnaires) was listed.

Individual Investors

Mean values of the responses of individual investors in the three countries to these questions are tabulated in the first two

Table 5.1
Mean values and T-test results—
Individual investors' views on the importance of corporate annual report items
(Buying decisions)

Corporate annual report items	$\bar{X}$ U.S.	$\bar{X}$ U.K.	$\bar{X}$ N.Z.	T (Probability) U.S. : U.K.	T (Probability) U.S. : N.Z.	T (Probability) U.K. : N.Z.
President's letter[a]	2.448	2.774	2.597	2.33 (.022)*	– .97 (.335)	.91 (.365)
Pictorial material	1.590	1.500	1.457	.98 (.329)	1.37 (.172)	.35 (.725)
Balance sheet	4.057	3.567	3.588	−3.56 (.001)**	2.80 (.006)**	– .10 (.922)
Income statement[b]	4.342	3.594	3.835	−5.58 (.000)**	3.61 (.001)**	−1.29 (.197)
Statement of changes in financial position	3.939	3.500	3.367	−3.08 (.003)**	3.64 (.000)**	.66 (.510)
Accounting policies	3.208	2.615	2.312	−3.83 (.000)**	6.01 (.000)**	1.51 (.132)
Other footnotes	3.227	2.046	2.266	−9.46 (.000)**	5.89 (.000)**	−1.17 (.244)
Auditor's report	3.002	2.548	2.250	−2.81 (.006)**	4.39 (.000)**	1.37 (.173)
Summary of operations for the last 5–10 years	4.190	3.677	3.901	−4.05 (.000)**	2.11 (.038)*	−1.26 (.209)
Management's discussion and analysis of the summary of operations	3.350	2.957	3.136	−2.90 (.004)**	1.36 (.178)	– .91 (.362)
Sales and income by product line[c]	3.464	2.934	3.052	−3.76 (.000)**	2.43 (.017)**	– .56 (.573)
Form 10-K report[d]	2.772	1.835	1.636	−6.75 (.000)**	8.42 (.000)**	1.18 (.239)

*Significant at levels of 0.05.
**Significant at levels of 0.05 and 0.01.
[a]"Chairman's letters" for questionnaires used in U.K. and N.Z.
[b]"Profit and loss account" for questionnaires used in U.K. and N.Z.
[c]"Sales and profit by product line" for questionnaires used in U.K. and N.Z.
[d]"Annual return filed with registrar of companies" for questionnaires used in U.K. and N.Z.

tables in this chapter, with the results of the T-test for buy decisions in table 5.1 and for hold/sell decisions in table 5.2.

Individual investors in the United States rated the income statement the most important part of the corporate annual report, with mean rating values of 4.34 for buying decisions and 4.36 for holding or selling decisions. They rated summaries of operations for the last five to ten years, balance sheet, and statements of changes in financial position very important, with mean rating values generally above 4. Sales and income by product line, management's discussion and analysis of the summary of operations, other footnotes, accounting policies, and auditor's reports were rated important, with mean rating values between 3 and 4. Form 10-K reports and presidents' letters were regarded as slightly important, with mean rating values between 2 and 3, while pictorial material was regarded as not important, with a mean rating value less than 2.

The S-N-K multiple range test of the difference in importance that individual investors placed on corporate annual report items

Table 5.2
Mean values and T-test results—
Individual investors' views on the importance of corporate annual report items
(Holding or selling decisions)

Corporate annual report items	$\bar{X}$			T (Probability)		
	U.S.	U.K.	N.Z.	U.S. : U.K.	U.S. : N.Z.	U.K. : N.Z.
President's letter[a]	2.586	3.044	3.068	3.19 (.002)**	−3.00 (.003)**	− .12 (.904)
Pictorial material	1.528	1.558	1.360	.29 (.772)	1.97 (.051)	1.61 (.110)
Balance sheet	4.051	3.667	3.632	−.279 (.006)**	2.52 (.013)*	.17 (.865)
Income statement[b]	4.357	3.681	3.932	−5.08 (.000)**	3.00 (.004)**	−1.35 (.180)
Statement of changes in financial position	4.055	3.556	3.581	−3.52 (.001)**	2.99 (.004)**	− .13 (.900)
Accounting policies	2.220	2.432	2.413	−5.31 (.000)**	5.18 (.000)**	.09 (.926)
Other footnotes	3.232	2.012	2.247	−9.42 (.000)**	6.14 (.000)**	−1.26 (.211)
Auditor's report	3.083	2.644	3.338	−2.64 (.009)**	4.06 (.000)**	1.34 (.183)
Summary of operations for the last 5–10 years	3.921	3.667	3.649	−1.82 (.071)	1.93 (.056)	.10 (.922)
Management's discussion and analysis of the summary of operations	3.369	3.079	3.189	−2.15 (.033)*	1.18 (.243)	− .58 (.561)
Sales and income by product line[c]	3.456	2.884	2.986	−3.83 (.000)**	2.71 (.008)**	− .47 (.636)
Form 10-K report[d]	2.767	1.773	1.722	−7.03 (.000)**	6.95 (.000)**	.28 (.781)

*Significant at levels of 0.05.
**Significant at levels of 0.05 and 0.01.
[a]"Chairman's letters" for questionnaires used in U.K. and N.Z.
[b]"Profit and loss account" for questionnaires used in U.K. and N.Z.
[c]"Sales and profit by product line" for questionnaires used in U.K. and N.Z.
[d]"Annual return filed with registrar of companies" for questionnaires used in U.K. and N.Z.

for buying decisions, shown in table 5.3, indicates that the importance of the income statement was significantly higher than any other item of the corporate annual report. Also, the importance of the balance sheet and statement of changes in financial position were significantly higher than any of the remaining lower-ranked items. The difference between the mean rating values of these two items was not statistically significant.

The same test performed for decisions to hold or sell shows similar results, with some exceptions (table 5.4). The importance investors placed on the income statement was significantly higher than that of any other item, but there were no statistically significant differences among the mean values of the importance placed on the balance sheet, the statement of changes in financial position, and the summary of operations for the last five to ten years.

Responses of individual investors in the United Kingdom and New Zealand indicate that they rated corporate annual report items almost identically. They rated the summary of operations

Table 5.3
Student-Newman-Keuls multiple range test for corporate annual report items (buying decisions)
Individual investors
The United States survey

Corporate annual report items (See key below.) — Mean differences — Multiple ranges

												α = .05	α = .01
A↘ ↙L	2.7557**											.2259	.2609
B↘ ↙K	2.5898**	1.8894**										.2224	.2574
C↘ ↙J	2.4516**	1.7235**	1.5991**									.2185	.2540
D↘ ↙I	2.3202**	1.5853**	1.4332**	1.3709**								.2141	.2500
E↘ ↙H	1.8410**	1.4539**	1.2950**	1.2050**	1.1290**							.2091	.2453
F↘ ↙G	1.7511**	.9747**	1.1636**	1.0668**	.9631**	1.1037**						.2032	.2400
G↘ ↙F	1.6520**	.8848**	.6844**	.9354**	.8249**	.9378**	1.0046**					.1963	.2335
H↘ ↙E	1.6267**	.7857**	.5945**	.4562**	.6935**	.7996**	.8387**	.9147**				.1877	.2257
I↘ ↙D	1.3848**	.7604**	.4954**	.3663**	.2143*	.6682**	.7005**	.7488**	.4355**			.1766	.2155
J↘ ↙C	1.1566**	.5185**	.4701**	.2672**	.1244	.1890*	.5691**	.6106**	.2696**	.3041**		.1608	.2013
K↘ ↙B	.8663**	.2903**	.2282**	.2419**	.0253	.0991	.0899	.4792**	.1314	.1382*	.1659*	.1342	.1774

*Significant at .05 level.
**Significant at .01 level.

Key to Corporate Annual Report Items		Mean Value
A	Income statement	4.3456
B	Summary of operations for the last 5–10 years	4.1797
[C	Balance sheet	4.0415
D]	Statement of changes in financial position	3.9101
[[E	Sales and income by product line	3.4309
F]	Management's discussion and analysis of the summary of operations	3.3410
G	Other footnotes	3.2419
H]	Accounting policies	3.2166
I	Auditor's report	2.9747
J	Form 10-K report	2.7465
K	President's letter	2.4562
L	Pictorial material	1.5899

[= Difference between mean values not significant.

for the last five to ten years and the profit and loss account very important (mean values of responses of nearly 4). These two groups of investors rated the balance sheet third in importance and the statement of changes in financial position fourth, followed by management's discussion of the summary of operations (mean values for all three items between 3 and 4). Sales and profit by product line, chairman's letter, accounting policies, auditor's report, other footnotes were considered somewhat important (having mean values between 2 and 3), while annual return filed with registrar of companies and pictorial material were considered not important (having mean values below 2).

Table 5.4
Student-Newman-Keuls multiple range test for corporate annual report items (holding or selling decisions)
Individual investors
The United States survey

Corporate annual report items (See key below.) — Mean differences

	L	K	J	I	H	G	F	E	D	C	B
A	2.8564**	1.7758**	1.6247**	1.2998**	1.1310**	1.1234**	1.0353**	.9521**	.4635**	.3577**	.3451**
B	2.5113**	1.4307**	1.2796**	.9547**	.7859**	.7783**	.6902**	.6070**	.1184	.0126	
C	2.4987**	1.4181**	1.2670**	.9421**	.7733**	.7657**	.6776**	.5944**	.1058		
D	2.3929**	1.3123**	1.1612**	.8363**	.6675**	.6599**	.5718**	.4886**			
E	1.9043**	.8237**	.6726**	.3744**	.1789	.1713	.0832				
F	1.8211**	.7405**	.5894**	.2645**	.0957	.0881					
G	1.7330**	.6524**	.5013**	.1764*	.0076						
H	1.7254**	.6448**	.4937**	.1688*							
I	1.5566**	.4760**	.3249**								
J	1.2317**	.1511*									
K	1.0806**										

Multiple ranges α = .05	α = .01
.2426	.2801
.2388	.2763
.2346	.2726
.2299	.2683
.2245	.2633
.2182	.2575
.2108	.2507
.2015	.2423
.1896	.2314
.1727	.2161
.1441	.1905

*Significant at .05 level.
**Significant at .01 level.

Key to Corporate Annual Report Items		Mean Value	Key to Corporate Annual Report Items		Mean Value
A	Income statement	4.3728	I	Auditor's report	3.0730
			J	Form 10-K report	2.7481
[B	Balance sheet	4.0277	K	President's letter	2.5970
C	Statement of changes in financial position	4.0151	L	Pictorial material	1.5164
D	Summary of operations for the last 5–10 years	3.9093			
[E	Sales and income by product line	3.4207			
F	Management's discussion and analysis of summary of operations	3.3375			
G	Other footnotes	3.2494			
H	Accounting policies	3.2418			

[= Difference between mean values not significant.

The T-test of significance performed on the responses of the three groups of individual investors produced the summary shown in table 5.5. Individual investors in the United States placed more importance on virtually all elements of corporate annual reports than did investors in the United Kingdom or New Zealand, between whom there were no significant differences.

Institutional Investors

Mean values and T-test results of responses of institutional investors are reported in table 5.6. United States investors rated the income statement, balance sheet, and statement of changes in financial position very important (mean values of 4.50, 4.48, and 4.26, respectively). They also rated summary of operations for the last five to ten years, accounting policies, and other footnotes very important (mean values above 4). Sales and income by product line, Form 10-K, the auditor's report, and management's discussion and analysis of the summary of operations were considered important (mean values between 3 and 4). The president's letter was considered slightly important (mean value between 2 and 3), while pictorial material was considered unimportant (mean value less than 2).

Table 5.7 shows the results of the S-N-K multiple range test performed on institutional investors' views on corporate annual report items for buying decisions. Investors placed significantly greater importance on the income statement than on all other corporate report items except the balance sheet. The importance they placed on the balance sheet was significantly higher than on all remaining corporate report items except the statement of changes in financial position.

Table 5.5
Comparative importance of corporate annual report items
Individual investors

U.S. : U.K.	More important
President's letter	U.K.
Balance sheet	U.S.
Income statement	U.S.
Statement of changes in financial position	U.S.
Accounting policies	U.S.
Other footnotes	U.S.
Auditor's report	U.S.
Summary of operations (buying)	U.S.
Management's discussion	U.S.
Sales and income by product line	U.S.
Form 10-K	U.S.
U.S. : N.Z.	**More important**
President's letter (holding/selling)	U.S.
Balance sheet	U.S.
Income statement	U.S.
Statement of changes in financial position	U.S.
Accounting policies	U.S.
Other footnotes	U.S.
Auditor's report	U.S.
Summary of operations (buying)	U.S.
Sales and income by product line	U.S.
Form 10-K	U.S.
U.K. : N.Z.	**More important**
None	

Table 5.6
Mean values and T-test results—
Institutional investors' views on the importance of corporate annual report items

	X̄			T and (Probability)		
	U.S.	U.K.	N.Z.	U.S. : U.K.	U.S. : N.Z.	U.K. : N.Z.
	President's letter[a]					
Buying decisions	2.654	3.390	3.262	4.66 (.000)**	3.62 (.000)	.70 (.488)
Holding or selling decisions	2.722	3.350	3.183	−3.74 (.000)**	2.53 (.013)*	.85 (.398)
	Pictorial material					
Buying decisions	1.503	1.388	1.400	−1.14 (.257)	−1.03 (3.07)	− .11 (.916)
Holding or selling decisions	1.493	1.380	1.373	−1.14 (.255)	−1.14 (.257)	.06 (.953)
	Balance sheet					
Buying decisions	4.456	4.583	3.984	1.36 (.175)	−3.68 (.000)**	4.59 (.000)**
Holding or selling decisions	4.500	4.622	3.918	1.34 (.181)	−4.05 (.000)**	4.77 (.000)**
	Income statement[b]					
Buying decisions	4.577	4.583	4.306	.07 (.944)	−2.40 (.018)*	2.28 (.025)*
Holding or selling decisions	4.607	4.585	4.210	− .23 (.821)	3.10 (.003)**	2.73 (.007)**
	Statement of changes in financial position					
Buying decisions	4.248	4.195	4.032	− .44 (.660)	−1.54 (.127)	1.07 (.288)
Holding or selling decisions	4.270	4.284	4.115	.11 (.912)	−1.10 (.274)	1.12 (.264)
	Accounting policies					
Buying decisions	4.125	3.762	3.226	−2.72 (.007)**	−5.61 (.000)**	3.01 (.003)**
Holding or selling decisions	4.122	3.780	3.230	−2.50 (.013)*	−5.21 (.000)**	2.96 (.004)**
	Other footnotes					
Buying decisions	4.178	3.712	3.082	−3.24 (.001)**	−6.29 (.000)**	3.17 (.002)**
Holding or selling decisions	4.172	3.692	3.067	−3.24 (.001)**	−6.11 (.000)**	3.09 (.003)**
	Auditor's report					
Buying decisions	3.585	3.012	2.344	−3.22 (.002)**	−6.31 (.000)**	2.93 (.004)**
Holding or selling decisions	3.541	3.250	2.233	−1.63 (.105)	−6.60 (.000)**	4.57 (.000)**
	Summary of operations for the last 5–10 years					
Buying decisions	4.144	3.446	3.645	−4.74 (.000)**	−2.95 (.004)**	−1.00 (.320)
Holding or selling decisions	3.905	3.099	3.317	−4.92 (.000)**	−3.10 (.003)**	−1.01 (.315)
	Management's discussion and analysis of the summary of operations					
Buying decisions	3.487	3.707	3.548	1.54 (.125)	.42 (.679)	.95 (.344)
Holding or selling decisions	3.517	3.638	3.475	.78 (.434)	− .25 (.801)	.85 (.396)
	Sales and income by product line[c]					
Buying decisions	3.869	3.531	3.290	− 2.24 (.026)*	−3.11 (.002)**	1.14 (.257)
Holding or selling decisions	3.784	3.575	3.133	−1.32 (.190)	−3.36 (.001)**	2.04 (.044)*

continued

Table 5.6 (continued)

	$\bar{X}$ U.S.	$\bar{X}$ U.K.	$\bar{X}$ N.Z.	T and (Probability) U.S. : U.K.	T and (Probability) U.S. : N.Z.	T and (Probability) U.K. : N.Z.
	Form 10-K report[d]					
Buying decisions	3.698	1.707	1.532	−13.50 (.000)**	−14.54 (.000)**	1.14 (.256)
Holding or selling decisions	3.630	1.753	1.492	−12.13 (.000)**	−14.02 (.000)**	1.68 (.096)

*Significant at level of 0.05.
**Significant at levels of 0.05 and 0.01.
[a]"Chairman's letters" for questionnaires used in U.K. and N.Z.
[b]"Profit and loss amount" for questionnaires used in U.K. and N.Z.
[c]"Sales and profit by product line" for questionnaires used in U.K. and N.Z.
[d]"Annual return filed with registrar of companies" for questionnaires used in U.K. and N.Z.

Table 5.7
Student-Newman-Keuls multiple range test for corporate annual report items (buying decisions)
Institutional investors
The United States survey

Corporate annual report items (See key below.) — Mean differences — Multiple ranges

	1	2	3	4	5	6	7	8	9	10	11		α = .05	α = .01
A↘												↙L		
B↘	3.0958**											↙K	.3289	.3798
C↘	2.9520**	1.9315**										↙J	.3235	.3748
D↘	2.7671**	1.7877**	1.1027**									↙I	.3182	.3697
E↘	2.6712**	1.6028**	.9589**	1.0548**								↙H	.3117	.3638
F↘	2.6712**	1.5069**	.7740**	.9110**	.9383**							↙G	.3044	.3571
G↘	2.6095**	1.5069**	.6781**	.7621**	.7945**	.7191**						↙F	.2959	.3492
H↘	2.3767**	1.4452**	.6781**	.6302**	.6096**	.5753**	.4863**					↙E	.2858	.3399
I↘	2.1575**	1.2124**	.6164**	.6302**	.5137**	.3904**	.3425*	.4246**				↙D	.2733	.3286
J↘	2.0410**	.9932**	.3836**	.5685**	.5137**	.2945*	.1576	.2808**	.4246**			↙C	.2571	.3138
K↘	1.9931**	.8767**	.1644	.3357**	.4520**	.2945**	.0617	.0959	.2808*	.3287**		↙B	.2342	.2930
	1.1643**	.8288**	.0479	.1165	.2192*	.2328*	.0617	.0000	.0959	.1849	.1438		.1954	.2583

*Significant at .05 level.
**Significant at .01 level.

Key to Corporate Annual Report Items		Mean Value	Key to Corporate Annual Report Items		Mean Value
A	Income statement	4.5890	G	Sales and income by product line	3.8699
B	Balance sheet	4.4452	H	Form 10-K report	3.6507
C	Statement of changes in financial position	4.2603	I	Auditor's report	3.5342
D	Other footnotes	4.1644	J	Management's discussion and analysis of the summary of operations	3.4863
E	Summary of operations for the last 5–10 years	4.1644	K	President's letter	2.6575
F	Accounting policies	4.1027	L	Pictorial material	1.4932

[= Difference between mean values not significant.

Table 5.8
Student-Newman-Keuls multiple range test for corporate annual report items (holding or selling decisions)
Institutional investors
The United States survey

Corporate annual report items (See key below.) — Mean differences

	L	K	J	I	H	G	F	E	D	C	B
A	3.1429**	1.8948**	1.1279**	1.0978**	1.0076**	.8271**	.6918**	.5188**	.4512**	.3534**	.1279
B	3.0150**	1.7669**	1.0000**	.9699**	.8797**	.6992**	.5639**	.3909**	.3233**	.2255*	
C	2.7895**	1.5414**	.7745**	.7444**	.6542**	.4737**	.3384**	.1654	.0978		
D	2.6917**	1.4436**	.6767**	.6466**	.5564**	.3759**	.2406	.0676			
E	2.6241**	1.3760**	.6091**	.5790**	.4888**	.3083*	.1730				
F	2.4511**	1.2030**	.4361**	.4060**	.3158*	.1353					
G	2.3158**	1.0677**	.3008*	.2707*	.1805						
H	2.1353**	.8872**	.1203	.0902							
I	2.0451**	.7970**	.0301								
J	2.0150**	.7669**									
K	1.2481**										

Multiple ranges

α = .05	α = .01
.3564	.4115
.3505	.4060
.3447	.4006
.3378	.3942
.3298	.3869
.3206	.3784
.3096	.3683
.2961	.3560
.2786	.3400
.2537	.3175
.2117	.2799

*Significant at .05 level.
**Significant at .01 level.

Key to Corporate Annual Report Items		Mean Value
[A	Income statement	4.6241
└ B	Balance sheet	4.4962
[C	Statement of changes in financial position	4.2707
D	Other footnoes	4.1729
└ E	Accounting policies	4.1053
[F	Summary of operations for the last 5–10 years	3.9323
└ G	Sales and income by product line	3.7970
[H	Form 10-K report	3.6165
I	Management's discussion and analysis of the summary of operations	3.5263
└ J	Auditor's report	3.4962
K	President's letter	2.7293
L	Pictorial material	1.4812

[= Difference between mean values not significant.

Results of the S-N-K test performed for holding or selling decisions (table 5.8) were identical except that the importance of the balance sheet was significantly greater statistically than that of the statement of changes in financial position. Institutional investors in the United Kingdom rated the balance sheet, profit and loss account, and statement of changes in financial position very important (mean values of 4.60, 4.58, and 4.24, respectively). Institutional investors in New Zealand, on the other hand, ranked the profit and loss account first (4.26), statement of changes in financial position second (4.07), and balance sheet third (3.95).

Institutional investors in the United Kingdom rated the following seven items important (mean values between 3 and 4): accounting policies, other footnotes, management's discussion and analysis of the summary of operations, sales and profits by product line, summary of operations for the last five to ten years, chairman's letter, and auditor's report. The annual return filed with registrar of companies and pictorial material were considered unimportant (mean values below 2).

Institutional investors in New Zealand, on the other hand, regarded six items important, in the following order: summary of operations for the last five to ten years, management's discussion and analysis of the summary of operations, sales and profits by product line, chairman's letter, accounting policies, and other footnotes. They rated the auditor's report as slightly important, and the annual report filed with registrar of companies and pictorial material as unimportant.

Table 5.9 summarizes the results of T-tests for significant differences between the three institutional investor groups on the importance of corporate annual report items. Institutional investors in the United Kingdom rated the chairman's letter signifi-

Table 5.9
Comparative importance of corporate annual report items
Institutional investors

U.S. : U.K.	More important
President's letter	U.K.
Accounting policies	U.S.
Other footnotes	U.S.
Auditor's report (buying)	U.S.
Summary of operations	U.S.
Sales and income by product line (buying)	U.S.
Form 10-K	U.S.
U.S. : N.Z.	**More important**
President's letter	N.Z.
All other items except pictorial material, statement of changes and management's discussion of operations	U.S.
U.K. : N.Z.	**More important**
Balance sheet	U.K
Profit and loss account	U.K.
Accounting policies	U.K.
Other footnotes	U.K.
Auditor's report	U.K.
Sales and income by product lines (buying)	U.K.

cantly more important than their counterparts in the United States, who found the account-based parts of the annual report (other than the financial statements) significantly more important than did the U.K. institutional investors. A similar result was found between institutional investors in the United States and New Zealand. Institutional investors in the United Kingdom in general rated the financial statements and related items more important than did N.Z. institutional investors.

Financial Analysts

Mean values and T-test results of the views of financial analysts on the importance of corporate annual report items are summarized in table 5.10. U.S. financial analysts, like institutional investors, regarded the income statement, balance sheet, and statement of changes in financial position the most important parts of corporate annual reports (mean values of 4.76, 4.60, and 4.35, respectively). They also regarded the following five items as very important (mean values above 4): accounting policies, sales and income by product line, summary of operations for the last five to ten years, other footnotes, and Form 10-K report. They regarded management's discussion and analysis of the summary of operations, auditor's report, and president's letter as important (mean values between 3 and 4), and pictorial material as not important (mean value less that 2).

Results of the S-N-K test (table 5.11) performed to analyze the U.S. financial analysts' responses for buying decisions indicate that the importance these analysts placed on the income statement had greater statistical significance than was evidenced for other corporate annual report items except the balance sheet, their second most important item. The importance of the balance sheet had a greater statistical significance than did the importance of the other corporate annual report items. The S-N-K test performed for holding or selling decisions produced essentially the same result (table 5.12).

Financial analysts in the United Kingdom rated the balance sheet most important (overall mean of 4.68, slightly higher than the profit and loss account mean of 4.62). New Zealand analysts, on the other hand, rated the profit and loss account the most important item (mean of 4.56, slightly higher than the balance sheet mean of 4.53).

Financial analysts in the United Kingdom also rated the statement of changes in financial position very important (mean value over 4), and the following five items important (mean values between 3 and 4): sales and profits by product line, management's discussion and analysis of the summary of operations, accounting policies, other footnotes, and chairman's letter. They rated summary of operations for the last five to ten years,

Table 5.10
Mean values and T-test results—
Financial analysts' views on the importance of corporate annual report items

	$\bar{X}$			T and (Probability)		
	U.S.	U.K.	N.Z.	U.S. : U.K.	U.S. : N.Z.	U.K. : N.Z.
	President's letter[a]					
Buying decisions	3.008	3.446	3.696	2.69 (.008)**	4.55 (.000)**	−1.49 (.139)
Holding or selling decisions	3.018	3.352	3.661	1.89 (.061)	3.99 (.000)**	−1.67 (.098)
	Pictorial material					
Buying decisions	1.622	1.338	1.407	−2.78 (.006)**	−1.75 (.083)	− .56 (.578)
Holding or selling decisions	1.550	1.278	1.310	−2.66 (.009)**	−2.09 (.038)*	− .30 (.768)
	Balance sheet					
Buying decisions	4.590	4.595	4.567	.04 (.966)	− .21 (.835)	.22 (.829)
Holding or selling decisions	4.613	4.764	4.492	1.65 (.101)	− .95 (.344)	2.01 (.047)*
	Income statement[b]					
Buying decisions	4.777	4.622	4.600	−1.59 (.115)	−1.78 (.079)	.17 (.863)
Holding or selling decisions	4.736	4.625	4.517	−1.09 (.277)	−1.95 (.054)	.82 (.416)
	Statement of changes in financial position					
Buying decisions	4.355	4.040	3.950	−2.16 (.033)*	−2.68 (.009)**	.51 (.611)
Holding or selling decisions	4.336	4.069	3.931	−1.75 (.083)	−2.65 (.009)**	.77 (.443)
	Accounting policies					
Buying decisions	4.198	3.554	3.525	−4.21 (.000)**	−3.80 (.000)**	.14 (.887)
Holding or selling decisions	4.218	3.611	3.500	−3.73 (.000)**	−3.81 (.000)**	.52 (.604)
	Other footnotes					
Buying decisions	4.138	3.486	3.561	−3.92 (.000)**	−3.24 (.002)**	− .37 (.715)
Holding or selling decisions	4.123	3.457	3.518	−3.88 (.000)**	−3.31 (.001)**	.29 (.773)
	Auditor's report					
Buying decisions	3.432	2.514	2.627	−4.54 (.000)**	−3.59 (.001)**	− .43 (.667)
Holding or selling decisions	3.413	3.014	2.544	−1.87 (.065)	−3.80 (.000)**	1.73 (.086)
	Summary of operations for the last 5–10 years					
Buying decisions	4.165	2.649	4.051	−9.51 (.000)**	− .74 (.464)	−7.09 (.000)**
Holding or selling decisions	3.991	2.611	3.897	−7.82 (.000)**	− .53 (.596)	−6.04 (.000)**
	Management's discussion and analysis of the summary of operations					
Buying decisions	3.667	3.808	3.983	1.02 (.310)	2.12 (.036)*	−1.09 (.277)
Holding or selling decisions	3.591	3.775	3.879	1.27 (.205)	1.82 (.071)	− .65 (.518)
	Sales and income by product line[c]					
Buying decisions	4.198	3.904	3.649	−2.16 (.032)*	−3.43 (.001)**	1.42 (.159)
Holding or selling decisions	4.144	3.887	3.464	−1.76 (.080)	−4.03 (.000)**	2.29 (.024)*

continued

Table 5.10 (continued)

	$\bar{X}$			T and (Probability)		
	U.S.	U.K.	N.Z.	U.S. : U.K.	U.S. : N.Z.	U.K. : N.Z.
	Form 10-K report[d]					
Buying decisions	4.078	2.216	1.644	−10.30 (.000)**	−14.20 (.000)**	2.77 (.006)**
Holding or selling decisions	3.952	2.342	1.534	−8.16 (.000)**	−14.75 (.000)**	3.97 (.000)**

*Significant at level of 0.05.
**Significant at levels of 0.05 and 0.01.
[a]"Chairman's letters" for questionnaires used in U.K. and N.Z.
[b]"Profit and loss account" for questionnaires used in U.K. and N.Z.
[c]"Sales and profit by product line" for questionnaires used in U.K. and N.Z.
[d]"Annual return filed with registrar of companies" for questionnaires used in U.K. and N.Z.

Table 5.11
Student-Newman-Keuls multiple range test for corporate annual report items (buying recommendations)
Financial analysts
The United States survey

Corporate annual report items (See key below.) — Mean differences — Multiple ranges

	Mean differences												Multiple ranges α = .05	α = .01
A↘	3.2000**											↙L	.3453	.3996
B↘	3.0190**	1.8191**										↙K	.3396	.3943
C↘	2.7619**	1.6381**	1.3143**									↙J	.3339	.3889
D↘	2.6762**	1.3810**	1.1333**	1.1048**								↙I	.3570	.3827
E↘	2.6190**	1.2953**	.8762**	.9238**	.6572**							↙H	.3194	.3755
F↘	2.5905**	1.2381**	.7905**	.6667**	.4762**	.6191**						↙G	.3104	.3671
G↘	2.5809**	1.2096**	.7333**	.5810**	.2191	.4381**	.6095**					↙F	.2998	.3573
H↘	2.5428**	1.2000**	.7048**	.5238**	.1334	.1810	.4285**	.5810**				↙E	.2866	.3452
I↘	2.0952**	1.1619**	.6952**	.4953**	.0762	.0953	.1714	.4000**	.5238**			↙D	.2696	.3296
J↘	1.8857**	.7143**	.6571**	.4857**	.0477	.0381	.0857	.1429	.3428**	.4381**		↙C	.2453	.3076
K↘	1.3809**	.5048**	.2095*	.4476**	.0381	.0096	.0285	.0572	.0857	.2571*	.1810	↙B	.2046	.2709

*Significant at .05 level.
**Significant at .01 level.

Key to Corporate Annual Report Items		Mean Value
┌A	Income statement	4.7524
└B	Balance sheet	4.5714
┌C	Statement of changes in financial position	4.3143
│D	Accounting policies	4.2286
│E	Sales and income by product line	4.1714
│F	Other footnotes	4.1429
│G	Summary of operations for the last 5–10 years	4.1333
└H	Form 10-K report	4.0952
I	Management's discussion and analysis of the summary of operations	3.6476
J	Auditor's report	3.4381
K	President's letter	2.933
L	Pictorial material	1.5524

[= Difference between mean values not significant.

Table 5.12
Student-Newman-Keuls multiple range test for corporate annual report items (holding or selling recommendations)
Financial analysts
The United States survey

Corporate annual report items (See key below.) — Mean differences

	L	K	J	I	H	G	F	E	D	C	B
A	3.2143**	1.7143**	1.2959**	1.1327**	.7449**	.7245**	.5612**	.5510**	.5000**	.3980**	.1123
B	3.1020**	1.6020**	1.1836**	1.0204**	.6326**	.6122**	.4489**	.4387**	.3877**	.2857*	
C	2.8163**	1.3163**	.8979**	.7347**	.3469*	.3265*	.1632	.1530	.1020		
D	2.7143**	1.2143**	.7959**	.6327**	.2449	.2245	.0612	.0510			
E	2.6633**	1.1633**	.7449**	.5817**	.1939	.1735	.0102				
F	2.6531**	1.1531**	.7347**	.5715**	.1837	.1633					
G	2.4898**	.9898**	.5714**	.4082**	.0204						
H	2.4694**	.9694**	.5510**	.3878**							
I	2.0816**	.5816**	.1632								
J	1.9184**	.4184**									
K	1.5000**										

Multiple ranges

α = .05	α = .01
.3755	.4351
.3692	.4292
.3631	.4234
.3557	.4164
.3472	.4087
.3375	.3995
.3258	.3888
.3115	.3756
.2929	.3585
.2666	.3345
.2222	.2945

*Significant at .05 level.
**Significant at .01 level.

Key to Corporate Annual Report Items		Mean Value
A	Income statement	4.7041
B	Balance sheet	4.5918
C	Statement of changes in financial position	4.3061
D	Accounting policies	4.2041
E	Sales and income by product line	4.1531
F	Other footnotes	4.1429
G	Summary of operations for the last 5–10 years	3.9796
H	Form 10-K report	3.9592
I	Management's discussion and analysis of the summary of operations	3.5714
J	Auditor's report	3.4082
K	President's letter	2.9898
L	Pictorial material	1.4898

[= Difference between mean values not significant. (Brackets in the key group A–B; C–F; D–H; I–J.)

auditor's report, and annual return filed with registrar of companies as slightly important, and pictorial material not important.

Financial analysis in New Zealand rated two corporate annual report items—summary of operations for the last five to ten years and management's discussion and analysis of the summary of operations—slightly more important than statement of changes in financial position (mean values all close to 4). They rated four other items as important (mean values between 3 and 4): chairman's letter, sales and profit by product line, other footnotes, and accounting policies. They rated the auditor's report as slightly important and the annual report filed with the registrar of companies as not important.

Table 5.13
Comparative importance of corporate annual report items
Financial analysts

U.S. : U.K.	More important
President's letter (buying)	U.K.
Pictorial material	U.S.
Statement of changes (buying)	U.S.
Accounting policies	U.S.
Other footnotes	U.S.
Auditor's report (buying)	U.S.
Summary of operations	U.S.
Sales and income by product line	U.S.
Form 10-K	U.S.
U.S. : N.Z.	**More important**
President's letter	N.Z.
Pictorial material (holding/selling)	U.S.
Statement of changes	U.S.
Accounting policies	U.S.
Other footnotes	U.S.
Auditor's report	U.S.
Management's discussion (buying)	U.S.
Sales and income by product line	U.S.
Form 10-K	U.S.
U.K. : N.Z.	**More important**
Balance sheet (holding/selling)	U.K.
Summary of operations	N.Z.
Sales and income by product line (holding/selling)	U.K.
Annual return	U.K.

Table 5.13 summarizes the results of the T-tests for significant differences between the three financial analyst groups on the importance of corporate annual report items. The U.S.-to-U.K. and U.S.-to-N.Z. comparisons resemble those for institutional investors, except that some additional account-based items were rated more important by financial analysts. There were fewer significant differences between U.K. and N.Z. financial analysts, and one item (summary of operations) was rated more important by New Zealand analysts.

Comparison of the Three User Groups

T-tests were performed on the data prepared for the three user groups. In the United States there were significant differences regarding nearly all items between individual investors and (a) institutional investors, and (b) financial analysts. Individual investors rated nearly all items less important. There were few significant differences between the ratings of institutional investors and financial analysts, although the latter gave higher importance to the income statement (buying), sales and income by product line, and the Form 10-K report.

The U.K. comparisons echoed the United States comparisons: significant differences between individual investors and the other two user groups on virtually all items, and differences between institutional investors and financial analysts only in regard to the summary of operations, sales and profit by product line (buying), and the annual return.

Analysis of the New Zealand data, however, gave results different from the United States and United Kingdom. The items rated significantly more important by New Zealand respondents were:

Individual investors	*Institutional investors*	*Financial analysts*
Pictorial material	Statement of changes in financial position	Chairman's letter
Annual return filed with registrar of companies		Balance sheet
		Profit & loss account
		Accounting policies
		Other footnotes
		Auditor's report
		Summary of operations
		Management's discussions
		Sales and profit by product line

We observed no identity of views between New Zealand institutional investors and financial analysts comparable to that observed in the other two countries.

Comparison of Buying and Holding/Selling Decisions for the Three User Groups

We also used T-tests to compare the significance of differences in rating the importance of corporate annual report items by the three user groups in relation to their buying decisions as opposed to their holding/selling decisions. In the United States, individual investors rated more important for hold/sell decisions the president's letter, the statement of changes, and the auditor's report. More important for buying decisions were pictorial material and the summary of operations. Institutional investors rated more important for buying decisions the summary of operations, sales and income by product line, and the Form 10-K report. Financial analysts rated only the summary of operations and the 10-K report more important for buying decisions.

For the United Kingdom, there were significant differences only in favor of:

Investor group	*Report item*	*Decision type*
Individual investors	Pictorial material	Hold/sell
	Accounting policies	Buy
Institutional investors	Auditor's report	Hold/sell
	Summary of operations	Buy
Financial analysts	Balance sheet	Hold/sell
	Auditor's report	Buy

There was even less significance in differences among the three user groups of New Zealand respondents. Individual investors rated the chairman's letter more important for hold/sell decisions. Institutional investors rated the profit and loss account, summary of operations, and sales and profit by product line all more important for buying decisions. Financial analysts rated pictorial material and sales and income by product line more important for buying decisions.

It is difficult to evaluate the results of these T-tests, but one conclusion appears supportable. The respondents generally rated important the financial statement parts of corporate annual report items for both buying and hold/sell decisions.

Ranking of Corporate Annual Report Items by the Three User Groups in All Three Countries

It is interesting to compare the rankings of corporate annual report items by the three user groups in the three countries. Table 5.14 shows a substantial identity of views among all respondents on the financial statement parts of corporate annual reports. Table 5.15 shows a similar, but not as consistent, pattern

Table 5.14
Ranking of corporate annual report items in order of relative importance
Financial statement parts

	United States			United Kingdom			New Zealand		
	Individual investors	Institutional investors	Financial analysts	Individual investors	Institutional investors	Financial analysts	Individual investors	Institutional investors	Financial analysts
Income statement	1	1	1	1	1	1	1	1	1
Balance sheet	2	2	2	2	1	1	2	3	2
Statement of changes in financial position	3	3	3	3	3	3	3	3	2
Accounting policies	5	5	4	5	5	4	4	4	4
Other footnotes	4	4	5	6	5	5	6	5	4
Auditor's report	6	6	6	4	6	6	5	6	6

Table 5.15
Ranking of corporate annual report items in order of relative importance
Other parts

	Individual investors			Institutional investors			Financial analysts		
	U.S.	U.K.	N.Z.	U.S.	U.K.	N.Z.	U.S.	U.K.	N.Z.
Summary of operations for the last 5–10 years	1	1	1	1	4	2	2	4	1
Sales and income by product line[a]	2	3	3	2	2	3	1	1	4
Management's discussion and analysis of summary of operations	3	2	2	4	1	1	4	2	2
Form 10-K report[b]	4	5	5	3	5	5	3	5	5
President's letter[c]	5	4	4	5	3	3	5	3	3
Pictorial material	6	6	6	6	6	6	6	6	6

[a]"Sales and profits by product line" in U.K. and N.Z.
[b]"Annual return filed with registrar of companies" in U.K. and N.Z.
[c]"Chairman's letter" in U.K. and N.Z.

of views on the other parts of the report. Only in regard to pictorial material were the nine groups in agreement; they all rated this information least important. It is noteworthy, however, that the annual returns filed with the registrar of companies under the relevant provisions of the company laws in the United Kingdom and New Zealand were rated of very little importance by respondents in those countries, and given far lower ratings than U.S. users gave to the Form 10-K.

Conclusion

The three user groups as a whole rated the financial statement parts of the corporate annual report higher than did institutional investors, and the latter higher than did individual investors. We regard these results as strong indirect evidence of the usefulness of financial statements for investment decisions and confirmatory of our second hypothesis (h_2), as stated in chapter 1. We also regard the higher ratings by the two professional groups as supporting our third hypothesis (h_3), that there are determinable differences in the importance of financial statements as viewed by different users. We shall examine the significance of this latter observation in chapters 8 and 9.

Anticipating our findings in those chapters, we postulate here a subgroup of individual investors resembling the professional user group in its need for financial statement information. Thus, if there is a case for differential disclosure, it should not mean supplying less financial statement information to individual investors. Rather, it means ensuring that each user group has all the information it needs for its investment decisions.

6 :: Investors' Views on the SEC's 10-K Report and on Interim Reporting

Our questionnaire included two questions designed to ascertain user views on the SEC's 10-K report and on corporate interim reports.

Part A: The SEC's 10-K Report

The three user groups in the United States were asked the following two questions about Form 10-K, which public companies must file annually with the SEC: "Are you aware that a 10-K report can be obtained from the company on request?" and "If your answer to the previous question was 'Yes,' how many times have you requested a 10-K report in the past year?"

For the three user groups in the United Kingdom and New Zealand, similar questions were asked: "Are you aware that an annual return can be inspected at the office of the Registrar of Companies on request?" and "If your answer to the previous question was 'Yes,' how many times in the past year have you inspected an annual return?"

Responses of the three user groups in the United States to the above questions are summarized in table 6.1. The majority of U.S. individual investors (81.3 percent) were aware that a 10-K report could be obtained from the company on request, and 44.3 percent of them did make such a request at least once during the preceding year.

Over 96 percent of U.S. institutional investors were aware that a 10-K report could be obtained from the company on request, and 54 percent had made such a request more than three times in the previous year. Over 93 percent of U.S. financial analysts were aware that a 10-K report could be requested, and 58 percent of them had made such requests more than three times in the previous year.

These findings confirm that corporate annual reports are not the only source of information used by investors and financial analysts.

T-tests for differences between the three groups' knowledge and use of Form 10-K reports were performed. As expected, no statistically significant differences appeared between institutional investors and financial analysts, but all the T-test values computed between individual investors and institutional inves-

Table 6.1
Investors and the 10-K report

	U.S.		U.K.		N.Z.	
	N	%	*N*	%	*N*	%
Individual investors						
Know that it is available	541	81.3	110	88.2	84	77.4
Used at least once in previous year	447	44.3	96	12.5	66	23.6
Institutional investors						
Know that it is available	164	96.3	83	97.6	63	98.4
Used at least once in previous year	155	65.5	81	35.8	62	51.6
Financial analysts						
Know that it is available	122	93.4	73	98.6	61	100.0
Used at least once in previous year	116	69.9	71	60.6	61	63.9

NOTE: U.K. and N.Z.—an annual return filed with the registrar of companies.

tors and between individual investors and financial analysts were significant at levels of both 0.05 and 0.01.

Over 88 percent of individual investors in the United Kingdom were aware that an annual return could be inspected at the office of the Registrar of Companies on request, but only 12.5 percent of them had made such an inspection in the previous year.

Almost 98 percent of U.K. institutional investors were aware that an annual return could be inspected, but a surprisingly low 35.8 percent had made at least one such inspection in the previous year. Of the U.K. financial analysts, 98.6 percent of them were aware that an annual return could be inspected, but only 40.6 percent had made such an inspection in the past year. The accessibility of annual returns to U.K. investors and analysts has been made more difficult in recent years, which may explain the U.K. percentage. That the annual return is not very informative may also be a factor.

Of the individual investors in New Zealand, 77.4 percent were aware that annual returns could be inspected at the registrar's office, but only 13.5 percent had made at least one such inspection in the previous year. Over 98 percent of N.Z. institutional investors were aware that annual returns could be inspected, but only slightly over 50 percent of them had made such an inspection in the previous year. All N.Z. financial analysts were aware of the availability of annual returns for inspection, and 63.9 percent of them made at least one such inspection in the previous year.

T-tests were performed to compare the responses of the three groups surveyed in the three countries, revealing no significant differences between individual investors. With reference to institutional investors, there was no significant difference in respect of awareness of the availability of 10-K reports (annual returns). United States institutional investors, however, reported significantly greater use of 10-K reports than their U.K. and N.Z. counterparts reported for the annual returns available to them.

There was a significant difference between N.Z. and U.S. financial analysts in respect of knowledge of the availability of 10-K reports (annual returns). A surprising 6.6 percent of United States financial analysts were not aware that the 10-K reports can be obtained from a company on request. Differences with regard to use of 10-K reports were even greater; United States analysts disclosed more use of 10-K reports than U.K. and N.Z. analysts reported of annual returns.

Part B: Interim Reporting

To provide empirical data on investors' views on and use of interim financial statements, the three user groups were asked the following questions:

Individual and Institutional Investors

"In making a decision about buying, holding or selling common stock,do you have the same degree of confidence in interim financial statements as in annual financial statements?"

Buying decisions			Holding or selling decisions		
Less confidence	Same	More confidence	Less confidence	Same	More confidence
1 2	3	4 5	1 2	3	4 5

"How many trades (buy and sell) have you made in the past year largely on information provided by interim financial statements?" (Please circle one)

None   1 to 5   6 to 10   Over 30

Financial analysts

"In making common stock investment recommendations, do you have the same degree of confidence in interim financial statements as in annual financial statements?"

Buying decisions			Holding or selling decisions		
Less confidence	Same	More confidence	Less confidence	Same	More confidence
1 2	3	4 5	1 2	3	4 5

Table 6.2
Relative confidence in interim financial statements

	U.S. Percentage	U.K. Percentage	N.Z. Percentage
Individual investors			
Rated less important	44.8	46.7	34.9
Rated same importance	48.6	45.7	56.3
Rated more important	6.6	7.6	8.7
Institutional investors			
Rated less important	53.7	62.7	69.8
Rated same importance	40.7	36.1	20.6
Rated more important	5.5	1.2	9.6
Financial analysts			
Rated less important	59.5	61.7	50.8
Rated same importance	37.2	30.1	35.6
Rated more important	3.3	8.2	13.6
Reliance on interim financial statements			
Individual investors[a]	34.5	24.8	35.0
Institutional investors[a]	61.4	77.2	49.2
Financial analysts[b]	70.8	86.6	98.2

NOTE: U.K. and N.Z.—half-yearly financial reports.
[a]Percentage having made at least one trade in preceding year based on interim information.
[b]Percentage reporting investment recommendations estimated to have been based on interim information during preceding year.

"What percentage of your common stock investment recommendations made in the last year do you estimate was based largely on information provided by interim financial statements?" (Please circle one)

None 1 to 5 6 to 20 21 to 50 Over 50

For questionnaires used in the United Kingdom and New Zealand, the phrase "interim financial statements" was replaced by "half-yearly financial reports." Responses of the three user groups in the three countries to the two questions are tabulated in table 6.2.

Relative Confidence

A substantial proportion of all U.S. groups reported that they had the same or more confidence in interim financial statements than in annual financial statements. Institutional investors as a group, however, had less confidence than did individual investors as a group, and financial analysts as a group had less confidence than did institutional investors as a group. All three groups reported less confidence in interim financial statements for buying decisions than for holding/selling decisions.

The responses of the three groups were compared using the T-test, revealing statistically significant differences in confidence between individual investors and institutional investors, and between individual investors and financial analysts. There were no statistically significant differences between institutional investors and financial analysts.

It appears that the three groups in the U.K. had even less confidence in half-yearly reports than the United States groups had in interim reports. Individual investors and financial analysts in New Zealand had slightly more confidence in the half-yearly financial reports, while the institutional investors in New Zealand had less confidence in these reports than their counterparts in the United Kingdom.

Use in Investment Decisions

One-third of individual investors in the United States reported one or more trades during the previous year based largely on interim financial statements: most of these investors (28.8 percent) reported 1 to 5 trades. Nearly two-thirds of the institutional investors reported trades based largely on interim financial statements during the previous year; 40 percent reported 1 to 5 trades. The financial analysts, however, reported even more reliance on interim financial statements; 70 percent disclosed that some of their recommendations were based on interim reports.

Compared to the U.S. groups' use of such information for investment decisions, a slightly lower percentage of individual investors in the United Kingdom reported that they relied on such information for making at least one trade during the preceding year, but a much higher percentage of institutional investors and financial analysts reported such reliance. In New Zealand, a higher percentage of individual investors and financial analysts relied on interim information for making trades. Over 98 percent of financial analysts in New Zealand had made at least one trade in the previous year based on the information provided by half-yearly reports, the highest percentage of any group in the thee countries. A much lower percentage (49.2) of institutional investors in New Zealand, on the other hand, reported such a trade in the preceding year.

T-tests revealed very few significant differences among the three groups in the three countries, even when calculated separately for buy versus hold/sell decisions. N.Z. individual investors disclosed significantly more confidence in half-yearly reports than did United States or United Kingdom individual investors in interim reports. N.Z. financial analysts disclosed more confidence than did U.K. financial analysts in interim financial statements. Regarding buy and hold/sell decisions, U.S. individual investors had more confidence than financial analysts for buy decisions, and N.Z. individual investors had more confidence than institutional investors for both buy and hold/sell decisions.

Conclusion

The answers to the questions about 10-K reports and annual returns reveal that investors and financial analysts use these sources in addition to annual corporate reports. Whether they look to them for additional financial information or for non-financial information not available in the annual report is a research question that must be addressed separately. It is noteworthy that institutional investors disclosed more knowledge about, and use of, these additional sources of information than did individual investors, and financial analysts disclosed more than did institutional investors. The answers also demonstrated the homogeneity of the institutional investor and financial analyst groups, and the heterogeneity of the individual investor groups.

The observation that substantially more use is made of 10-K reports in the United States than of annual returns in the United Kingdom and New Zealand suggests that a comparative study of the information content of these two types of filing should be undertaken to see if the explanation lies in the availability of substantially more information in the 10-K report.

With reference to interim reporting, it appears as if, on the whole, all user groups had less confidence in interim financial statements than in corporate annual reports, even though a substantial minority in each group reported having the same or more confidence. In spite of this reduced confidence, a significant number of respondents in all three groups reported the use of interim financial statements in making investment decisions or recommendations. Again, we noted more differences between the individual investor groups than between the other two groups.

Further research should attempt to identify the reasons for the relative lack of confidence in interim financial statements, and also to study the specific use made of such statements, particularly by financial analysts, who reported a large proportion of investment recommendations resulting from the information contained in them.

7 :: Investors' Views on the Importance of Published Forecast Information

The SEC and Company Projections

The SEC in early administrative decisions assumed a tolerant posture toward the inclusion of projections in filing with the Commission, but by 1939 it had arrived at a general policy that predictions of future economic performance were not permitted in such filings. Public companies conformed to this policy but nevertheless issued projections to the investment community in press releases and even in annual corporate reports. (This section uses material from the appendix to the *Report of the Advisory Committee on Corporate Disclosure to the Securities and Exchange Commission* 2:A265–329.)

Following increasing pressure upon the SEC to regulate projection disclosure, and to facilitate the extension of the practice, the SEC initiated a public rule-making proceeding on 1 November 1972. The proceeding was ordered for the purpose of gathering information relevant to a reassessment of the SEC's policy. Critics of this policy argued that company forecasts were the real key to the present value of securities, were significant factors affecting security prices, and provided highly relevant information for investment decisions. Critics argued against discriminatory practices in this area, in the interests of efficient allocation of capital through the medium of securities markets.

Between 1973 and 1976 the SEC published a number of conclusions and proposals on this subject but was unable to decide whether disclosure of projections should be made mandatory. A detailed 1975 proposal was withdrawn in 1976 in the face of widespread opposition from the business and investment communities. In announcing the withdrawal of the proposed rule and form changes, the SEC stated that "the Commission will not object to disclosure in filings with the Commission of projections which are made in good faith and have a reasonable basis, provided that they are presented in an appropriate format and accompanied by information adequate for investors to make their own judgments."

In accordance with this change in policy, the SEC amended Rule 14a-9 to delete the reference to predictions of "earnings" as possibly misleading in certain situations; neither encouraged nor discouraged the making and filing of projections; and issued Proposed Guide 62, "Disclosure of Projections of Future Economic Performance," announcing that the guide would be used by the Commission's staff in reviewing filings.

To provide empirical answers to the question of whether published forecast information is useful for equity investment decisions, a section on published forecasts was included in the questionnaires for this study. The three user groups were asked to evaluate the usefulness for investment decisions of seven forecast items if they were to be regularly published in financial statements: next year's sales, cost of goods sold, expenses, earnings ("profits" for U.K. and N.Z. questionnaires), cash flow, dividends, and additions to plant and equipment.

Individual Investors

The mean values of the responses of individual investors in the three countries to this question are tabulated in table 7.1, and the results of the T-tests are shown, separated as to buy and hold/sell decisions.

Individual investors in all three countries ranked "earnings forecast for next year" as the most useful item and "dividends forecast for next year" as the second most useful item. There were differences between the three groups in ranking the other five items. U.S. investors ranked cash flow forecast third and additions to plant and equipment forecast fourth. U.K. investors ranked additions to plant and equipment forecast third and cash flow forecast fourth. New Zealand investors, on the other hand, ranked sales revenue forecast third, expenses forecast fourth, and cash flow forecast fifth. All three groups ranked the cost of goods sold forecast last.

The differences in the mean values given to the seven forecast items by all three groups were not large. In the United States, all seven of the items forecast had mean values between 3 and 4. The most useful forecast information, earnings for next year, had a mean value of 3.89 while the least useful forecast, cost of goods sold for next year, had a mean of 3.05.

The mean values of the first five items for U.K. individual investors were between 3 and 4. Profit forecast for next year, the most useful item, had a mean value of 3.85 while cost of goods sold and expenses for next year, the least useful items, had mean values between 2 and 3.

It is interesting to compare these ratings to those for published corporate annual report items for these same groups of investors. For individual investors in the United States, for example, the four most important corporate annual report items had mean values above 4 while the next item, sales and income by product line, had a much lower mean value of 3.46. If the

Table 7.1
Mean values and T-test results—individual investors' views on the usefulness of forecast information

	$\bar{X}$			T and (Probability)		
	U.S.	U.K.	N.Z.	U.S. : U.K.	U.S. : N.Z.	U.K. : N.Z.
	Sales revenue forecast for next year					
Buying decisions	3.370	3.232	2.425	−1.00 (.321)	− .36 (.719)	−1.01 (.316)
Holding or selling decisions	3.406	3.165	3.350	−1.73 (.087)	.38 (.705)	− .99 (.323)
	Cost of goods sold forecast for next year					
Buying decisions	3.039	2.766	2.747	−1.89 (.061)	2.02 (.046)*	.10 (.920)
Holding or selling decisions	3.054	2.808	2.886	−1.69 (.093)	1.09 (.276)	− .40 (.693)
	Expenses forecast for next year					
Buying decisions	3.218	2.830	3.240	−2.73 (.007)**	− .15 (.882)	−2.10 (.037)*
Holding or selling decisions	3.221	2.837	3.205	−2.73 (.007)**	.10 (.918)	−1.89 (.060)
	Profits forecast for next year					
Buying decisions	3.860	3.697	3.788	−1.24 (.216)	.49 (.623)	− .49 (.624)
Holding or selling decisions	3.886	3.802	3.949	− .67 (.503)	− .44 (.662)	− .83 (.407)
	Cash flow forecast for next year					
Buying decisions	3.425	3.237	3.141	−1.25 (.212)	1.82 (.072)	.47 (.637)
Holding or selling decisions	3.432	3.258	3.104	−1.15 (.254)	2.09 (.039)	.75 (.454)
	Dividends forecast for next year					
Buying decisions	3.491	3.515	3.763	.18 (.860)	−2.09 (.039)*	−1.44 (.150)
Holding or selling decisions	3.509	3.541	3.772	.24 (.814)	−1.97 (.051)	−1.33 (.186)
	Additions to plant and equipment forecast for next year					
Buying decisions	3.369	3.255	3.112	− .83 (.409)	1.67 (.098)	.73 (.464)
Holding or selling decisions	3.337	3.210	3.101	− .90 (.369)	1.50 (.136)	.55 (.581)

*Significant at level of 0.05.
**Significant at levels of 0.05 and 0.01.

mean values can be used as a general guide, it can be inferred that investors in the United States regarded an earnings forecast as less useful than the four above-mentioned published corporate annual report items, but more useful than the remaining eight published items. A comparison of the mean values given to published (historical) annual report items and forecast information items by individual investors in the United States is provided in table 7.2.

For individual investors in the United Kingdom, the most important published corporate annual report items—the summary of operations for the last five to ten years and the profit and loss account—had mean values of 3.67 and 3.64 respectively, and the profit forecast for the next year had a mean value of 3.75. Hence it may be inferred that U.K. investors regarded a profit forecast for the next year as more useful than any published corporate annual report item. The second most useful item, dividends forecast for next year, was rated as more useful than nine of the corporate annual report items, with a mean value of 3.53. A comparison of the mean values of published corporate annual report items with the mean values of forecast information items for U.K. individual investors is provided in table 7.3.

Individual investors in New Zealand rated the profit and loss account and summary of operations for the last 5 to 10 years the most important corporate annual report items, with mean values of 3.88 and 3.78, respectively. The most useful forecast item, profit forecast for next year, had a mean value of 3.87. It may be inferred that these investors regarded a profit forecast and a profit and loss account as equally useful, and more useful than the other published corporate annual report items. The second

Table 7.2
Mean values of corporate annual report items and forecast items
Individual investors
The United States survey

Corporate annual report items	$\bar{X}$	Forecast items	$\bar{X}$
Income statement	4.35		
Summary of operations for the last 5 to 10 years	4.05		
Balance sheet	4.05		
Statement of changes in financial position	4.00		
		Earnings forecast for next year	3.87
		Dividends forecast for next year	3.50
Sales and income by product line	3.46		
		Cash flow forecast for next year	3.43
		Sales revenue forecast for next year	3.38
Management's discussion and analysis of the summary of operations	3.36		
		Additions to plant and equipment forecast for next year	3.35
Other footnotes	3.23		
		Expense forecast for next year	3.22
Accounting policies	3.21		
Auditor's report	3.05	Cost of goods sold forecast for next year	3.05
Form 10-K report	2.76		
President's letter	2.52		
Pictorial material	1.56		

Table 7.3
Mean values of corporate annual report items and forecast items
Individual investors
The United Kingdom survey

Corporate annual report items	$\bar{X}$	Forecast items	$\bar{X}$
		Profits forecast for next year	3.75
Summary of operations for the last 5 to 10 years	3.67		
Profit and loss account	3.64		
Balance sheet	3.62		
Statement of changes in financial position	3.53	Dividends forecast for next year	3.53
		Cash flow forecast for next year	3.25
		Additions to plant and equipment forecast for next year	3.23
		Sales revenue forecast for next year	3.14
Management's discussion and analysis of the summary of operations	3.02		
Sales and profits by product line	2.91		
Chairman's letter	2.91		
		Expense forecast for next year	2.83
		Cost of goods sold forecast for next year	2.79
Auditor's report	2.60		
Accounting policies	2.52		
Other footnotes	2.03		
Annual return filed with registrar of companies	1.80		
Pictorial material	1.53		

most useful forecast item, dividends forecast for next year (mean value of 3.77), was regarded as more useful than ten of the published corporate annual report items. A comparison of the mean values of published corporate annual report items with those of forecast information items for New Zealand individual investors is provided in table 7.4.

Institutional Investors

Mean values and T-test results of the responses of institutional investors in the three countries to the question regarding the usefulness of forecast items are tabulated in table 7.5.

Institutional investors in all three countries rated the earnings forecast as the most useful forecast item and the cash flow forecast second. Rankings for the next five forecast items, however, differed widely.

A close examination of the ratings given to the forecast items by the three national groups revealed interesting results. Institutional investors in the United States, like individual investors in that country, rated all forecast items important (mean values between 3 and 4). The most useful forecast item, earnings forecast for next year, had a mean value of 3.70 while the last ranked item, cost of goods sold forecast, had a mean value of 3.31, only 0.39 lower.

Compared to the mean values for U.S. institutional investors' importance of published corporate annual report items, it was found that these investors rated seven of the corporate annual items more useful than the earnings forecast, the most useful forecast item. The two least important published items, the president's letter and pictorial material, were rated less useful than the least useful forecast item. A comparison of the mean values

Table 7.4
Mean values of corporate annual report items and forecast items
Individual investors
The New Zealand survey

Corporate annual report items	$\bar{X}$	Forecast items	$\bar{X}$
Profit and loss account	3.88		
		Earnings forecast for next year	3.87
Summary of operations for the last 5 to 10 years	3.78		
		Dividend forecast for next year	3.77
Balance sheet	3.61		
Statement of changes in financial position	3.47		
		Sales revenue forecast for next year	3.39
		Expenses forecast for next year	3.22
Management's discussion and analysis of the summary of operations	3.16		
		Cash flow forecast for next year	3.12
		Additions to plant and equipment forecast for next year	3.11
Sales and profits by product line	3.02		
Chairman's letter	2.83		
		Cost of goods sold forecast for next year	2.82
Accounting policies	2.36		
Auditor's report	2.27		
Other footnotes	2.27		
Form 10-K report	1.68		
Pictorial material	1.41		

Table 7.5
Mean values and T-test results—
Institutional investors' views on the usefulness of forecast information

	X			T and (Probability)		
	U.S.	U.K.	N.Z.	U.S. : U.K.	U.S. : N.Z.	U.K. : N.Z.
	Sales revenue forecast for next year					
Buying decisions	3.462	3.872	3.623	2.57 (.011)**	.98 (.330)	1.34 (.183)
Holding or selling decisions	3.487	3.883	3.627	2.50 (.013)*	.81 (.420)	1.33 (.186)
	Cost of goods sold forecast for next year					
Buying decisions	3.273	3.590	3.367	1.98 (.049)*	.53 (.597)	1.14 (.256)
Holding or selling decisions	3.338	3.610	3.397	1.69 (.092)	.32 (.746)	1.08 (.281)
	Expenses forecast for next year					
Buying decisions	3.360	3.487	3.443	.78 (.439)	.47 (.638)	.23 (.822)
Holding or selling decisions	3.413	3.533	3.475	.71 (.476)	.34 (.736)	.29 (.775)
	Profits forecast for next year					
Buying decisions	3.671	4.259	4.197	3.97 (.000)**	3.33 (.001)**	.39 (.700)
Holding or selling decisions	3.719	4.275	4.237	3.79 (.000)**	3.30 (.001)**	.24 (.813)
	Cash flow forecast for next year					
Buying decisions	3.558	4.215	3.918	4.50 (.000)**	2.32 (.022)*	1.84 (.067)
Holding or selling decisions	3.533	4.231	3.915	4.76 (.000)**	2.31 (.022)*	1.87 (.064)
	Dividends forecast for next year					
Buying decisions	3.445	4.185	4.852	5.09 (.000)**	2.50 (.014)*	1.88 (.063)
Holding or selling decisions	3.480	4.125	3.867	4.34 (.000)**	2.36 (.020)*	1.40 (.165)
	Additions to plant and equipment forecast for next year					
Buying decisions	3.523	3.500	3.180	− .17 (.868)	−2.18 (.031)*	1.86 (.065)
Holding or selling decisions	3.471	3.487	3.220	.12 (.906)	−1.56 (.122)	1.54 (.126)

*Significant at level of 0.05.
**Significant at levels of 0.05 and 0.01.

of all published annual report and forecast information items for U.S. institutional investors is provided in table 7.6.

Institutional investors in the United Kingdom rated three forecast items—profit, cash flow, and dividends—very useful (mean values above 4), and the other four items useful (mean values between 3 and 4).

Compared with the ratings of published corporate annual report items, the mean value of 4.27 for the profit forecast was lower than those of only two of the published items—the balance sheet and the profit and loss account. The second most useful forecast item, cash flow forecast, was also regarded as more useful than ten of the published items, while the third, dividends forecast, was regarded as more useful than nine of the published items. It may be stated that U.K. institutional investors regarded forecast items as more useful than did their counterparts in the United States. A comparison of the mean values of all published annual report and forecast information items for U.K. institutional investors is provided in table 7.7.

Institutional investors in N.Z. rated the profit forecast very useful (mean value being above 4), and the other six forecast items useful (mean values between 3 and 4).

Compared with ratings of published corporate annual report items, the mean value of 4.27 for the profit forecast was lower than those of the published balance sheet and profit and loss account items. The second most useful forecast item, cash flow forecast, was also regarded as more useful than ten of the published items, while the third, dividends forecast, was regarded as more useful than nine of the published items. It may be stated that the New Zealand institutional investors, like their counterparts in the United Kingdom, considered forecast information more useful than did their counterparts in the United States. A

Table 7.6
Mean values of corporate annual report items and forecast items
Institutional investors
The United States survey

Corporate annual report items	$\bar{X}$	Forecast items	$\bar{X}$
Income statement	4.59		
Balance sheet	4.48		
Statement of changes in financial position	4.26		
Other footnotes	4.18		
Accounting policies	4.12		
Summary of operations for the last 5 to 10 years	4.03		
Sales and income by product line	3.83		
		Earnings forecast for next year	3.70
Form 10-K report	3.66		
Auditor's report	3.56		
		Cash flow forecast for next year	3.55
Management's discussion and analysis of the summary of operations	3.50	Additions to plant and equipment forecast for next year	3.50
		Sales revenue forecast for next year	3.48
		Dividends forecast for next year	3.46
		Expenses forecast for next year	3.39
		Cost of goods sold forecast for next year	3.31
President's letter	2.69		
Pictorial material	1.50		

Table 7.7
Mean values of corporate annual report items and forecast items
Institutional investors
The United Kingdom survey

Corporate annual report items	$\bar{X}$	Forecast items	$\bar{X}$
Balance sheet	4.60		
Profit and loss account	4.58		
		Profit forecast for next year	4.27
Statement of changes in financial position	4.24		
		Cash flow forecast for next year	4.22
		Dividend forecast for next year	4.16
		Sales revenue forecast for next year	3.88
Accounting policies	3.77		
Other footnotes	3.70		
Management's discussion and analysis of the summary of operations	3.67		
		Cost of goods sold forecast for next year	3.60
Sales and profits by profit line	3.55		
		Expenses forecast for next year	3.51
		Additions to plant and equipment for next year	3.49
Chairman's letter	3.37		
Summary of operations for the last 5 to 10 years	3.27		
Auditor's report	3.13		
Annual return filed with registrar companies	1.73		
Pictorial material	1.38		

comparison of the mean values of all published annual report and forecast information items for New Zealand institutional investors is provided in table 7.8.

Financial Analysts

Mean values and T-test results of responses of financial analysts in the three countries to the question of the usefulness of forecast items are tabulated in table 7.9.

Financial analysts in the United States ranked cash flow and earnings forecast equally useful, while their counterparts in the United Kingdom ranked profit forecast first and cash flow forecast second. The New Zealand analysts ranked profit forecast first and dividends forecast second. The rankings of the seven forecast items by the three groups of analysts differed more than those by the individual and institutional investors.

Financial analysts in the United States as a group, like individual and institutional investors, rated all seven forecast items as useful (mean values between 3 and 4). The most useful forecast items, cash flow and earnings forecasts, both had mean values of 3.91, while the last-ranked forecast item, dividends forecast, had a mean value of 3.63. There was a difference of only 0.28 between these mean values.

Comparing these results with the group's views on the importance of published corporate annual report items, it was found that the mean values (3.91) of the most useful forecast item, cash flow forecast for the next year, was lower than the mean values of eight of the published report items. The least useful forecast item, however, dividends forecast, was more useful than the other four published items. A comparison of the mean values of all published annual report and forecast information items for U.S. financial analysts is provided in table 7.10.

Table 7.8
Mean values of corporate annual report items and forecast items
Institutional investors
The New Zealand survey

Corporate annual report items	$\bar{X}$	Forecast items	$\bar{X}$
Profit and loss account	4.26		
		Profit forecast for next year	4.22
Statement of changes in financial position	4.07		
Balance sheet	3.95		
		Cash flow forecast for next year	3.92
		Dividend forecast for next year	3.86
		Sales revenue forecast for next year	3.63
Management's discussion and analysis of the summary of operations	3.51		
Summary of operations for the last 5 to 10 years	3.48		
		Expenses forecast for next year	3.46
		Cost of goods sold forecast for next year	3.38
Accounting policies	3.23		
Chairman's letter	3.22		
Sales and profits by product line	3.21		
		Additions to plant and equipment forecast for next year	3.20
Other footnotes	3.08		
Auditor's report	2.29		
Form 10-K report	1.51		
Pictorial material	1.39		

Table 7.9
Mean values and T-test results—financial analysts' views on the usefulness of forecast information

	$\bar{X}$			T (Probability)		
	U.S.	U.K.	N.Z.	U.S. : U.K.	U.S. : N.Z.	U.K. : N.Z.
	Sales revenue forecast for next year					
Buying decisions	3.723	3.822	4.254	.59 (.553)	3.56 (.001)**	−2.42 (.017)*
Holding or selling decisions	3.726	3.863	4.152	.81 (.418)	2.62 (.010)**	−1.51 (.134)
	Cost of goods sold forecast for next year					
Buying decisions	3.638	3.743	3.448	.65 (.520)	− .98 (.331)	1.38 (.172)
Holding or selling decisions	3.631	3.797	3.379	1.00 (.317)	−1.24 (.219)	1.89 (.062)
	Expenses forecast for next year					
Buying decisions	3.800	3.859	3.593	.38 (.703)	−1.24 (.217)	1.40 (.164)
Holding or selling decisions	3.864	3.930	3.525	.43 (.668)	−1.94 (.055)	2.04 (.044)*
	Profits forecast for next year					
Buying decisions	3.931	4.378	4.500	3.23 (.001)**	4.41 (.000)**	− .92 (.357)
Holding or selling decisions	3.893	4.319	4.534	2.96 (.004)**	4.98 (.000)**	−1.54 (.126)
	Cash flow forecast for next year					
Buying decisions	3.958	4.137	3.898	1.29 (.199)	− .38 (.704)	1.41 (.161)
Holding or selling decisions	3.867	4.206	3.930	2.38 (.018)*	.38 (.703)	1.57 (.119)
	Dividends forecast for next year					
Buying decisions	3.626	3.824	4.322	1.21 (.226)	4.41 (.000)**	−2.86 (.005)**
Holding or selling decisions	3.639	3.824	4.203	1.12 (.265)	3.29 (.001)**	−2.03 (.045)*
	Additions to plant and equipment forecast for next year					
Buying decisions	3.708	3.311	3.492	−2.55 (.012)*	−1.43 (.157)	−1.03 (.304)
Holding or selling decisions	3.661	3.297	3.339	−2.25 (.026)*	−1.90 (.060)	− .21 (.831)

*Significant at level of 0.05.
**Significant at levels of 0.05 and 0.01.

Financial analysts in the United Kingdom as a group rated two forecast items, profit and cash flow forecasts, as very useful (mean values above 4) and the other five items useful (mean values between 3 and 4).

Compared with the mean values of published corporate annual report items, profit and cash flow forecasts were rated more useful than ten of the published report items; the profit and loss account and balance sheet had higher mean values, however. The next four forecast items—expenses, dividends, sales revenue, and cost of goods sold—had higher mean values than seven of the published items. A comparison of the mean values of all published annual report and forecast information items for U.K.

financial analysts is provided in table 7.11. It is clear from these results that U.K. financial analysts, like U.K. individual investors, regarded forecast information as more useful than did their counterparts in the United States.

Financial analysts in New Zealand as a group rated three forecast items—profit, dividends, and sales revenue—very important (mean values above 4). The other four forecast items all had mean values well above 3. Compared with the mean values of published corporate annual report items, the profit forecast was rated almost as useful as the profit and loss account and balance sheet. Dividends and sales revenue forecasts were rated more useful than the other ten published corporate annual report items. A comparison of the mean values of all published annual report and forecast information items for New Zealand financial analysts is provided in table 7.12. Like their counterparts in the United Kingdom, financial analysts in New Zealand regarded

Table 7.10
Mean values of corporate annual report items and forecast items
Financial analysts
The United States survey

Corporate annual report items	$\bar{X}$	Forecast items	$\bar{X}$
Income statement	4.76		
Balance sheet	4.60		
Statement of changes in financial position	4.35		
Accounting policies	4.21		
Sales and income by product line	4.17		
Other footnotes	4.13		
Summary of operations for the last 5 to 10 years	4.08		
Form 10-K report	4.02		
		Cash flow forecast for next year	3.91
		Earnings forecast for next year	3.91
		Expenses forecast for next year	3.83
		Sales revenue forecast for next year	3.73
		Additions to plant and equipment forecast for next year	3.69
		Cost of goods sold forecast for next year	3.64
Management's discussion and analysis of the summary of operations	3.63	Dividends forecast for next year	3.63
Auditor's report	3.42		
President's letter	3.01		
Pictorial material	1.59		

Table 7.11
Mean values of corporate annual report items and forecast items
Financial analysts
The United Kingdom survey

Corporate annual report items	$\bar{X}$	Forecast items	$\bar{X}$
Balance sheet	4.68		
Profit and loss account	4.62		
		Profit forecast for next year	4.34
		Cash flow forecast for next year	4.16
Statement of changes in financial position	4.08		
Sales and profits by product line	3.88	Expenses forecast for next year	3.88
		Sales revenue forecast for next year	3.83
		Dividends forecast for next year	3.81
Management's discussion and analysis of the summary of operations	3.80		
		Cost of goods sold forecast for next year	3.75
Accounting policies	3.59		
Other footnotes	3.49		
Chairman's letter	3.39		
		Additions to plant and equipment forecast for next year	3.28
		Published statements by company directors	2.97
Auditor's report	2.75		
Summary of operations for the last 5 to 10 years	2.60		
Annual return filed with registrar of companies	2.30		
Pictorial material	1.31		

forecast information, as compared to published corporate annual report items, more useful than did their counterparts in the United States.

Table 7.13 summarizes the rankings of forecast information items by the three user groups in the three countries. A general consistency of rankings prevailed, in spite of the differences commented upon above. The respondents' ratings did not vary significantly when the importance of forecast information for buying decisions was compared with its importance for hold/sell decisions.

It is interesting that the three user groups in the United States rated most historical financial statement items more important than forecast information, whereas the three United Kingdom and New Zealand user groups rated forecast information more

Table 7.12
Mean values of corporate annual report items and forecast items
Financial analysts
The New Zealand survey

Corporate annual report items	$\bar{X}$	Forecast items	$\bar{X}$
Profit and loss account	4.56		
Balance sheet	4.53		
		Profit forecast for next year	4.52
		Dividends forecast for next year	4.26
		Sales revenue forecast for next year	4.20
Summary of operations for the last 5 to 10 years	3.97		
Statement of changes in financial position	3.94		
Management's discussion and analysis of the summary of operations	3.93		
		Cash flow forecast for next year	3.91
Chairman's letter	3.68		
		Published statements by company directors	3.65
		Expenses forecast for next year	3.56
Sales and profits by product line	3.56		
Other footnotes	3.54		
Accounting policies	3.51		
		Additions to plant and equipment forecast for next year	3.42
		Cost of goods sold forecast for next year	3.41
Auditor's report	2.59		
Form 10-K report	1.59		
Pictorial material	1.36		

Table 7.13
Ranking of forecast information items in order of relative importance

	United States			United Kingdom			New Zealand		
	Individual investors	Institutional investors	Financial analysts	Individual investors	Institutional investors	Financial analysts	Individual investors	Institutional investors	Financial analysts
Earnings	1	1	1	1	1	1	1	1	1
Dividends	2	5	6	2	3	5	2	3	2
Cash flow	3	2	1	3	2	2	5	2	4
Additions to plant and equipment	4	3	5	4	7	7	6	7	6
Sales revenue	5	4	4	5	4	4	3	4	3
Expenses	6	6	3	6	6	3	4	5	5
Cost of goods sold	7	7	6	7	5	6	7	6	7

important than such historical information. Several possible explanations for this difference of attitude can be hypothesized:

> Users in the United States may perceive published financial statements as being more reliable than do users in the United Kingdom and New Zealand.
>
> Corporate annual reports published in the United States may contain more financial information than do those published in the United Kingdom and New Zealand.
>
> Conditions in the United Kingdom and New Zealand at the time may have made historical information less valuable than forecast information. For example, a high rate of inflation would tend to direct investors' attention to the future and minimize the importance of past results.
>
> Users in the three countries may differ in their level of sophistication. For example, the United Kingdom and New Zealand respondents may have been, on the average, better educated in finance and therefore placed more reliance on present value approaches to security analysis.

Only the last of these possible explanations can be investigated through the medium of the responses themselves. It will be considered further in chapter 8.

Comparison Between Populations Sampled

Tables 7.1, 7.5, and 7.9 showed the results of T-tests performed to compare the significance of differences between the various groups of respondents' attitudes to forecasts. There were some significant differences in mean values between individual investors in the United States and New Zealand regarding the cost of goods sold forecast (buying decisions) and the cash flow forecast (hold/sell decisions), which United States investors rated more important, and dividends forecast (buy decisions), rated more important by New Zealand investors.

The only other significant difference had to do with the expenses forecast, which United States and New Zealand individual investors rated more important than did United Kingdom investors, but New Zealand investors only in relation to the buy decision.

The T-tests performed between other groups of individual and institutional investors and financial analysts did not add to the preceding observations.

Conclusion

We found that United States investors and financial analysts, as groups, rated important all forecast items on which they were asked to comment. They rated the financial statement parts of corporate annual reports even more important, however, which suggests that U.S. investors and financial analysts like to make their own forecasts but would welcome corporate forecasts, perhaps as a check on their own figures.

Investors and financial analysts in the United Kingdom and New Zealand, on the other hand, rated some forecast items more important than financial statement information. We have suggested some possible explanations for this difference and regard it as a suitable field for further research.

8 :: Characteristics of User Groups

As a step toward developing a taxonomy of users of financial statements (investors and financial analysts), the questionnaires used for this study contained questions about the backgrounds and investment activities of respondents. Individual investors were asked for information on the following topics:

1) Amount of portfolio
2) Amount of common stock in portfolio
3) Experience in common stock investment
4) Trades made in past year
5) Annual income
6) Age
7) Education level
8) Major in college
9) Occupation
10) Formal training in accounting, finance or investment.

Institutional investors were asked questions about the following topics:

1) Amount of portfolio managed
2) Amount of common stock in portfolio
3) Trades made in past year
4) Experience in occupation
5) Title in firm
6) University degree in business
7) Education in accounting
8) Education in finance or investment analysis

Financial analysts were asked about the following things:

1) University degree in business
2) Education in accounting
3) Education in finance or investment analysis
4) Experience as financial analyst
5) Main activity

Individual Investors

The characteristics of U.S. individual investors surveyed are summarized in tables 8.1, 8.2, and 8.3. Of the individual investors responding, 74.9 percent were within the age group 35–64, while 21 percent were 65 and older. Annual income ranged from under $10,000 to over $80,000, with 74.7 percent of the respondents having annual incomes over $40,000. They reported a wide variety of occupations. Only 11.9 percent of the respondents were retired, unemployed, or stated other occupations, such as "housewife."

In terms of size of portfolio, 68.1 percent held over $50,000 of investments; 60.7 percent had over $50,000 in common stock investments. More than five years' experience in common stock investing was reported by 96.7 percent of the respondents. Over 64 percent reported having executed between one and nine transactions during the preceding year; 15.2 percent reported none, and 20.6 percent had made 10 or more transactions.

Over 95 percent of respondents had some form of college education; 81.1 percent held undergraduate or graduate degrees. The proportion reporting some graduate work was 43.8

Table 8.1
Individual investor characteristics—investment activity
The United States survey

Amount of portfolio owned			Experience in common stock investment		
	N	%		*N*	%
$1– $999	6	1.2	Under 1 year	1	0.2
$1,000– $9,999	52	10.3	1–4 years	17	3.1
$10,000–$49,999	103	20.4	5–9 years	63	11.7
$50,000–$99,999	83	16.4	10–19 years	160	29.5
$100,000 and over	261	51.7	20 years and over	301	55.5
No information given	49*		No information given	12*	
Total	554	100.0	Total	554	100.0
Amount of common stock in portfolio			**Trades made in the past year**		
	N	%		*N*	%
$1– $999	14	2.8	None	81	1.52
$1,000– $9,999	61	12.1	1– 9	343	64.2
$10,000–$49,999	121	24.0	10–19	65	12.2
$50,000–$99,999	88	17.4	20–49	35	6.6
$100,000 and over	221	43.7	50 and over	10	1.8
No information given	49*		No information given	20*	
Total	554	100.00	Total	554	100.0

*Not included in the calculation of percentages.

Table 8.2
Individual investor characteristics—personal
The United States survey

Age	N	%	Annual income**	N	%
Under 35	23	4.1	Under $10,000	5	0.4
35–44	53	9.9	$10,000–$19,999	16	3.2
45–54	158	29.3	$20,000–$39,999	110	21.7
55–64	192	35.7	$40,000–$79,999	214	42.2
65 and older	113	21.0	$80,000 and over	165	32.5
No information given	16*		No information given	47*	
TOTAL	554	100.0	TOTAL	554	100.0

Occupation	Number	Percentage
Bankers	54	10.0
CPA—accountants	15	2.8
Stockbroker	4	0.8
Executive—finance	77	14.4
Insurance agents	7	1.3
Presidents and vice presidents	102	19.0
Manager	34	6.3
Executive—other	92	17.2
Small business	6	1.1
Physicians and scientists	1	0.2
Attorney	17	3.2
Teacher (education)	1	0.2
Other professionals	35	6.5
Sales (salesmen; sales representatives)	4	0.8
Retired, unemployed, housewives	64	11.9
Other	23	4.3
No information given	18*	
TOTAL	554	100.00

*Not included in the calculation of percentages.

percent. Of those who stated their major field of study, 52.8 percent had majored in business administration or accounting. Also, 64.3 percent reported having had some formal education or training in accounting, finance, or stock market investing.

Characteristics of U.K. and N.Z. individual investors are tabulated in tables 8.4 through 8.9. Table 8.10 provides an overview of the personal characteristics identified by the respondents to the four surveys—Florida, United States, United Kingdom, and New Zealand.

Tables 8.11 through 8.13 provide results of additional chi-square tests performed to test the significance of differences between characteristics of the different groups of individual investors. These results indicate statistically significant differences between United States and U.K. respondents (9 significant values out of 10) and United States and N.Z. respondents (9 out of 10). However, the U.K. and N.Z. respondents were less dissimilar, as there were only 5 statistically significant values in the chi-square test performed. No statistically significant differences emerged regarding annual income, educational background, and number of respondents with majors in accounting and business administration, with investment-related occupation, and with formal training in finance, accounting, or investments.

The U.K. and N.Z. respondents had significantly lower annual incomes than the U.S. respondents. In terms of size of port-

Table 8.3
Individual investor characteristics—education
The United States survey

Education level	Number	Percentage
Less than high school graduate	8	1.5
High school graduate	18	3.4
Some college	75	14.0
College graduate	200	37.3
Postgraduate work	235	43.8
No information given	18*	
TOTAL	554	100.0

Major in college	Number	Percentage
Accounting	64	11.6
Business administration	228	41.2
Education	4	0.7
Liberal arts	19	3.4
Sciences	23	4.2
Engineering	69	12.5
Law	41	7.4
Medicine	4	0.6
Others	8	1.4
Less than high school graduate, high school graduate, and no information given	94	17.0
TOTAL	554	100.0

Formal education or training in accounting, finance, or stock market investing	Number	Percentage
Yes	348	64.7
No	190	35.3
No information given	16*	
TOTAL	554	100.0

*Not included in the calculation of percentages.

Table 8.4
Individual investor characteristics—investment activity
The United Kingdom survey

Amount of portfolio owned**	N	%	Experience in ordinary share investment	N	%
£1– £499	5	5.0	Under 1 year	0	0.0
£500– £4,999	21	21.0	1–4 years	1	0.9
£5,000–£24,999	52	52.0	5–9 years	14	12.8
£25,000–£49,999	10	10.0	10–19 years	39	35.8
£50,000 and over	12	12.0	20 years and over	55	50.5
No information given	13*	____	No information given	4*	____
TOTAL	113	100.0	TOTAL	113	100.0
Amount of ordinary shares in portfolio**	N	%	**Trades made in the past year**	N	%
£1– £499	8	8.0	None	27	25.2
£500– £4,999	25	25.0	1– 9	71	66.4
£5,000–£24,999	46	46.0	10–19	6	5.6
£25,000–£49,999	11	11.0	20–49	2	1.9
£50,000 and over	10	10.0	50 and over	1	0.9
No information given	13*	____	No information given	6*	____
TOTAL	113	100.00	TOTAL	113	100.0

*Not included in the calculation of percentages.
**Exchange rate around 1977 was £1 = $1.73.

folios and investment in common stocks, the U.K. respondents had much smaller portfolios and investment than the U.S. respondents, and the N.Z. respondents even smaller.

The U.K. and N.Z. respondents had a significantly lower educational background than the U.S. respondents. The number having some training in finance or accounting and investment-related employment was much lower for the U.K. and N.Z. samples than for the United States samples. Similarly, the number of respondents having had a college major in accounting and business administration was much lower for the United Kingdom and New Zealand than for the United States.

The U.K. respondents were significantly older, but the N.Z. respondents were significantly younger, than the U.S. respondents. In terms of experience in common stock investment, there were no statistically significant differences between the United States and U.K. samples, but the N.Z. sample had less experience. In terms of activity in trading, there were no statistically significant differences between the U.S. and N.Z. respondents, but the U.K. respondents reported fewer trades in the previous year.

Table 8.5
Individual investor characteristics—personal
The United Kingdom survey

Age	N	%	Annual income**	N	%
Under 35	3	3.1	Under £2,999	20	20.2
35–44	5	5.2	£3,000–£5,999	34	34.3
45–54	21	21.9	£6,000–£11,999	35	35.4
55–64	26	27.1	£12,000–£23,999	9	9.1
65 and older	41	42.7	£24,000 and over	1	1.0
No information given	17*		No information given	14*	
TOTAL	113	100.0	TOTAL	113	100.0

Occupation	Number	Percentage
University professor—accounting	4	3.8
Bankers	2	1.9
Stockbroker	0	0.0
Executive—finance	1	1.0
Insurance agents	1	1.0
Presidents and vice presidents	7	6.7
Manager	7	6.7
Executive—other	2	1.9
Small business	1	1.0
Physicians and scientists	1	1.0
Attorney	0	0.0
Teacher (education)	1	1.0
Other professionals	5	4.8
Sales (salesmen; sales representatives)	8	7.7
Retired, unemployed, housewives	59	56.7
Other	5	4.8
No information given	9*	
TOTAL	113	100.00

*Not included in the calculation of percentages.
**Exchange rate around January 1977 was £1 = $1.73.

It will be noted that none of the surveys asked the sex of respondents. It appears as if the majority of respondents were male, but a relatively larger number in New Zealand reported the occupation of "housewife."

Institutional Investors and Financial Analysts

The characteristics of these groups in the United States are tabulated in tables 8.14 through 8.18.

The magnitude of the impact of institutional investors on the U.S. stock market is revealed by this sample. While 48.3 percent of U.S. individual investors responding had portfolios under $100,000, 67.5 percent of institutional investors surveyed had portfolios over $10 million. While 56.7 percent of individual in-

Table 8.6
Individual investor characteristics—education
The United Kingdom survey

Education level	Number	Percentage
Less than high school graduate	47	44.8
High school graduate	12	11.4
Some college	13	12.4
College graduate	26	24.8
Postgraduate work	7	6.6
No information given	8*	
TOTAL	113	100.0

Major in college	Number	Percentage
Accounting	1	3.6
Business administration	3	10.7
Education	0	0.0
Liberal arts	5	17.9
Sciences	3	10.7
Engineering	5	17.9
Law	4	14.2
Medicine	2	7.1
Others	5	17.9
Less than high school graduate, high school graduate, and no information given	85*	
TOTAL	113	100.0

Formal educational training in accounting, finance, or stock market investing	Number	Percentage
Yes	29	26.4
No	81	73.6
No information given	3*	
TOTAL	113	100.0

*Not included in the calculation of percentages.

vestors had under $100,000 in common stock investments, 52.9 percent of the institutional investors had over $10 million in common stock. While 64.2 percent of the individual investors made between one and nine transactions during the previous year, almost 46 percent of the institutional investors made over 50 transactions in the same time period.

Individual investors in the United States are apparently a heterogeneous group, but institutional investors and financial analysts are more alike. Almost 81 percent of U.S. institutional investors and 85.4 percent of U.S. financial analysts had degrees in business. The great majority of them had a formal training in accounting and finance.

Table 8.7
Individual investor characteristics—investment activity
The New Zealand survey

Amount of portfolio owned	N	%	Experience in common stock investment	N	%
$1– $999	11	13.4	Under 1 year	0	0.0
$1,000– $9,999	33	40.2	1–4 years	5	5.9
$10,000–$49,999	28	34.2	5–9 years	31	36.5
$50,000–$99,999	6	7.3	10–19 years	27	31.8
$100,000 and over	4	4.9	20 years and over	22	25.8
No information given	3*		No information given	0	
TOTAL	85	100.0	TOTAL	85	100.0

Amount of common stock in portfolio	N	%	Trades made in the past year	N	%
$1– $999	15	18.8	None	19	22.6
$1,000– $9,999	35	43.7	1– 9	44	52.4
$10,000–$49,999	24	30.0	10–19	14	16.6
$50,000–$99,999	2	2.5	20–49	5	6.0
$100,000 and over	4	5.0	50 and over	2	2.4
No information given	5*		No information given	1*	
TOTAL	85	100.00	TOTAL	85	100.0

*Not included in the calculation of percentages.

The characteristics of institutional investors in the United Kingdom and New Zealand are tabulated in tables 8.19 through 8.24.

The dominance of the stock market by institutional investors is even more striking in the United Kingdom. We found that 87.5 percent of the U.K. institutional investors had portfolios over £10 million, 89.6 with £5 million or more in common stock, while 88 percent of individual investors in the U.K. had portfolios less than £50,000, 90 percent with less than £50,000 in common stocks. Further, 93.6 percent of institutional investors in the United Kingdom had made more than 50 trades in the previous year, while 91.6 percent of individual investors had made fewer than 10 trades in the same period.

Institutional investors in New Zealand had smaller portfolios and investment in common stock than their counterparts in the United States and the United Kingdom. The three groups' investment activity is summarized in table 8.25.

As far as educational background was concerned, 46.2 percent of U.K. institutional investors, and 40 percent of N.Z. institutional investors had university degrees in business. It was not possible to analyze their formal training in accounting and

Table 8.8
Individual investor characteristics—personal
The New Zealand survey

Age	N	%	Annual income**	N	%
Under 35	11	17.7	Under $5,000	25	31.6
35–44	11	17.7	$5,000–$9,999	17	21.5
45–54	9	14.5	$10,000–$19,999	28	35.5
55–64	19	30.7	$20,000–$39,999	6	7.6
65 and older	12	19.4	$40,000 and over	3	3.8
No information given	23*		No information given	6*	
TOTAL	85	100.0	TOTAL	85	100.0

Occupation	Number	Percentage
University professor—accounting	0	0.0
CPA—accountants	5	6.1
Stockbroker	1	1.2
Executive—finance	2	2.4
Insurance agents	0	0.0
Presidents and vice presidents	2	2.4
Manager	4	4.9
Executive—other	3	3.7
Small business	1	1.2
Physicians and scientists	10	12.2
Attorney	0	0.0
Teacher (education)	6	7.3
Other professionals	0	0.0
Sales (salesmen; sales representatives)	1	1.2
Retired, unemployed, housewives	32	39.0
Other	15	18.4
No information given	3*	
TOTAL	85	100.00

*Not included in the calculation of percentages.

finance in terms of college work since many of them did not give this information.

The characteristics of financial analysts in the United Kingdom and New Zealand are given in tables 8.26 and 8.27. Over 79 percent of the analysts in the U.K. characterized themselves as security analysts while 63 percent of the analysts in New Zealand characterized themselves as investment counselors. The professional activity, experience, and educational background of financial analysts in the three countries are summarized in table 8.28.

In terms of educational background, 50 percent of U.K. financial analysts had a university degree in business, while 46.6 percent of N.Z. analysts had such a degree. Again, it was not possible to analyze these groups' formal training in terms of accounting and finance courses taken, since very few of them gave such information.

The homogeneity of the U.S. professional user groups (institutional investors and financial analysts) is revealed by a comparison of their educational backgrounds and training in accounting, finance, and investment analysis (table 8.29).

(*Text continued on page 95*)

Table 8.9
Individual investor characteristics—education
The New Zealand survey

Education level	Number	Percentage
Less than university entrance	28	33.3
University entrance	8	9.5
Some university courses	18	21.4
University graduate	22	26.3
Postgraduate work	8	9.5
No information given	1*	
TOTAL	85	100.0

Major in college	Number	Percentage
Accounting	7	20.6
Business administration	4	11.8
Education	1	2.9
Liberal arts	5	14.7
Sciences	9	26.5
Engineering	7	20.6
Law	1	2.9
Medicine	0	0.0
Less than high school graduate, high school graduate, and no information given	51*	
TOTAL	85	100.0

Formal education training in accounting, finance, or stock market investing	Number	Percentage
Yes	26	31.7
No	56	68.3
No information given	3*	
TOTAL	85	100.0

*Not included in the calculation of percentages.

Table 8.10
Individual investor characteristics

	Percentage of respondents		
	U.S.	U.K.	N.Z.
1. Age			
Under 44	14.0	8.3	35.4
45–65	65.0	49.0	45.2
65 and older	21.0	42.7	19.4
2. Annual income			
Under $5,000	—	20.2	31.6
$5,000– $9,999	0.4	34.3	21.5
$10,000–$19,999	3.2	35.4	35.5
$20,000–$39,999	21.7	9.1	7.6
$40,000 and over	74.7	1.0	3.8
3. Occupation			
Investment related	54.6	21.1	17.0
Not related	45.4	78.9	83.0
4. Amount of portfolio owned			
Less than $10,000	11.5	26.0	53.6
$10,000–$49,999	20.4	52.0	34.2
$50,000–$99,999	16.4	10.0	7.3
Over $100,000	51.7	12.0	4.9
5. Amount invested in common stocks			
Less than $10,000	14.9	33.0	62.5
$10,000–$49,999	24.0	46.0	30.0
$50,000–$99,999	17.4	11.0	2.5
Over $100,000	43.7	10.0	5.0
6. Experience in common stock investment			
Under 5 years	3.3	0.9	5.9
5– 9 years	11.7	12.8	36.5
10–19 years	29.5	35.8	31.8
20 years and more	55.5	50.5	25.8
7. Trades made in the past year			
None	15.2	25.2	22.6
1– 9	64.2	66.4	52.4
10–19	12.2	5.6	16.6
Over 20	8.4	2.8	8.4
8. Education			
Less than high school	1.5	44.8	33.3
High school graduate	3.4	11.4	9.5
Some university	14.0	12.4	21.4
Graduates	81.1	31.4	35.8
9. Major in college			
Accounting or business administration	52.8	14.3	32.4
Other	47.2	85.7	67.6
10. Training in finance or accounting			
Yes	64.3	26.4	31.7
No	35.7	73.6	68.3

Table 8.11
Chi-square values to compare personal characteristics of United States and United Kingdom individual investors

Personal characteristics	Chi-square values	Degrees of freedom	Significance
Size of investment portfolio	78.80	4	.0000**
Size of common stock investment in portfolio	58.05	4	.0000**
Length of experience in common stock investing	3.56	4	.4693
Number of trades in the previous twelve months	12.74	4	.0126*
Size of annual income	248.88	4	.0000**
Level of education	240.52	4	.0000**
Major in college	26.88	2	.0000**
Age	21.63	4	.0002**
Experience in finance or accounting	97.30	4	.0000**
Formal training in finance, accounting, or investments	53.55	1	.0000**

*Significant at level of 0.05.
**Significant at levels of 0.05 and 0.01.

Table 8.12
Chi-square values to compare personal characteristics of United States and New Zealand individual investors

Personal characteristics	Chi-square values	Degrees of freedom	Significance
Size of investment portfolio	124.52	4	.0000**
Size of common stock investment in portfolio	116.09	4	.0000**
Length of experience in common stock investing	44.84	4	.0000**
Number of trades in the previous twelve months	5.46	4	.2436*
Size of annual income	233.29	4	.0000**
Level of education	160.76	4	.0000**
Major in college	18.65	2	.0001**
Age	24.49	4	.0001**
Experience in finance or accounting	90.13	4	.0000**
Formal training in finance, accounting, or investments	30.97	1	.0000**

*Significant at level of 0.05.
**Significant at levels of 0.05 and 0.01.

Table 8.13
Chi-square values to compare personal characteristics
of United Kingdom and New Zealand individual investors

Personal characteristics	Chi-square values	Degrees of freedom	Significance
Size of investment portfolio	15.49	4	.0038**
Size of common stock investment in portfolio	17.51	4	.0015**
Length of experience in common stock investing	22.79	3	.0000**
Number of trades in the previous twelve months	9.92	4	.0417*
Size of annual income	6.43	4	.1690
Level of education	4.54	4	.3375
Major in college	4.12	2	.1273
Age	19.30	4	.0007**
Experience in finance or accounting	2.31	4	.6781
Formal training in finance, accounting, or investments	.42	1	.5165

*Significant at level of 0.05.
**Significant at levels of 0.05 and 0.01.

Table 8.14
Institutional investor characteristics—investment activity
The United States survey

Amount of portfolio owned	Number	Percentage
$1– $9,999	1	.6
$10,000– $99,999	7	4.5
$100,000– $999,999	17	11.0
$1,000,000–$9,999,999	25	16.2
$10,000,000 and over	104	67.5
No information given	11*	
TOTAL	165	100.0

Amount of common stock portfolio**	Number	Percentage
$1– $9,999	3	1.9
$10,000– $99,999	11	7.1
$100,000– $999,999	24	15.5
$1,000,000–$9,999,999	35	22.6
$10,000,000 and over	82	52.9
No information given	10*	
TOTAL	165	100.0

Trades made in the past year	Number	Percentage
None	8	5.0
1– 9	24	15.1
10–19	32	20.1
20–49	22	13.9
50 and over	73	45.9
No information given	6*	
TOTAL	165	100.0

*Not included in the calculation of percentages.

Table 8.15
Institutional investor characteristics—
Title and experience of official responsible for investment decisions
The United States survey

Title in firm	Number	Percentage
Chairman of the board	5	3.2
President	45	28.5
Vice president	55	34.8
Treasurer	11	7.0
Investment manager or portfolio manager	20	12.6
Financial analyst	6	3.8
Director of research	4	2.5
Controller or assistant controller	3	1.9
Secretary	2	1.3
Other titles	7	4.4
No information given	7*	
TOTAL	165	100.0

Experience in common stock investment	Number	Percentage
4 years or less	10	6.4
5– 9 years	26	16.6
10–19 years	53	33.7
20–39 years	60	38.2
40 years and over	8	5.1
No information given	8*	
TOTAL	165	100.0

*Not included in the calculation of percentages.

Table 8.16
Institutional investor characteristics—
Education and training of official responsible for investment decisions
The United States survey

University degree in business

	Number	Percentage
Yes	131	80.9
No	31	19.1
No information given	3*	
TOTAL	165	100.0

Training in accounting

Quarter hours	Number	Percentage
None	16	11.2
1–5	11	7.7
6–15	53	37.0
16–30	35	24.5
More than 30	28	19.6
No information given	22*	
TOTAL	165	100.0

Training in finance, investment analysis, financial analysis, or stock market investing

Quarter hours	Number	Percentage
None	16	11.3
1–5	8	5.6
6–15	52	36.6
16–30	35	24.6
More than 30	31	21.9
No information given	23*	
TOTAL	165	100.0

*Not included in the calculation of percentages.

Table 8.17
Financial analyst characteristics—
Professional activity and experience
The United States survey

Professional activity	Number	Percentage
Security analyst	42	34.1
Fund or money manager	43	35.0
Investment counselor	20	16.3
Financial executive	2	1.6
Financial consultant	4	3.3
Stockbroker	1	0.8
Other	11	8.9
TOTAL	123	100.0

Experience as financial analyst	Number	Percentage
4 years or less	5	4.1
5– 9 years	22	18.0
10–19 years	51	41.8
20–39 years	34	27.9
40 years and over	10	8.2
No information given	1*	
TOTAL	123	100.0

*Not included in the calculation of percentages

(*Text continued from page 89*)

Conclusion

The findings reported in this chapter, together with the observations at the conclusions of chapters 6 and 7, bear directly on hypotheses h_4 and h_5, namely:

—Institutional investors and financial analysts are homogeneous user groups
—Individual investors are not a homogeneous user group

It appears that not only are the two professional user groups homogeneous, but they also resemble each other closely with respect to the educational qualifications that equip them for the use of financial statements in investment decisions. Individual investors, on the other hand, are very dissimilar.

These differences will be further investigated in chapter 9, with the objective of determining if there are recognizable subgroups of individual investors, and if so, if one of them resembles the two professional user groups in its use of financial statements for investment decisions.

Table 8.18
Financial analyst characteristics—
Education and training
The United States survey

University degree in business	Number	Percentage
Yes	105	85.4
No	18	14.6
Total	123	100.0

Training in accounting		
Quarter hours	Number	Percentage
None	11	10.0
1–5	16	14.6
6–15	37	33.6
16–30	35	31.8
More than 30	11	10.0
No information given	13*	
Total	123	100.0

Training in finance, investment analysis, financial analysis, or stock market investing		
Quarter hours	Number	Percentage
None	11	10.3
1–5	6	5.6
6–15	38	35.5
16–30	32	29.9
More than 30	20	18.7
No information given	16*	
Total	123	100.0

*Not included in the calculation of percentages.

Table 8.19
Institutional investor characteristics—investment activity
The United Kingdom survey

Amount of portfolio managed**	Number	Percentage
£1– £4,999	0	0.0
£5,000– £49,999	1	2.1
£50,000– £499,999	0	0.0
£500,000–£4,999,999	5	10.4
£5,000,000 and over	42	87.5
No information given	36*	
TOTAL	84	100.0

Amount of ordinary shares in portfolio**	Number	Percentage
£1– £4,999	0	0.0
£5,000– £49,999	1	2.1
£50,000– £499,999	0	0.0
£500,000–£4,999,999	4	8.3
£5,000,000 and over	43	89.6
No information given	36*	
TOTAL	84	100.0

Trades made in the past year	Number	Percentage
None	0	0.0
1– 9	0	0.0
10–19	1	2.1
20–49	2	4.3
50 and over	44	93.6
No information given	37*	
TOTAL	84	100.0

*Not included in the calculation of percentages.
**Exchange rate around January 1977 was £1 = $1.73.

Table 8.20

Institutional investor characteristics—Education, title, and experience
The United Kingdom survey

Title in firm	Number	Percentage
Investment manager or portfolio manager	28	60.9
Director of research	2	4.3
Other titles	16	34.8
No information given	38*	
TOTAL	84	100.0

Experience in ordinary share investment	Number	Percentage
Under 5 years	4	8.7
5– 9 years	18	39.0
10–19 years	17	36.9
20–39 years	6	13.1
40 years and over	1	2.2
No information given	38*	
TOTAL	84	100.0

*Not included in the calculation of percentages

Table 8.21
Institutional investor characteristics—
Education and training of official responsible for investment decisions
The United Kingdom survey

University degree in business

	Number	Percentage
Yes	12	46.2
No	14	53.8
No information given	58*	
Total	84	100.0

Training in accounting

Quarter hours	Number	Percentage
None	33	71.7
1–5	8	17.4
6–15	3	6.5
16–30	2	4.4
More than 30	0	0.0
No information given	38*	
Total	84	100.0

Training in finance, investment analysis,
financial analysis, or stock market investing

Quarter hours	Number	Percentage
None	31	66.0
1–5	8	17.0
6–15	4	8.5
16–30	4	8.5
More than 30	0	0.0
No information given	37*	
Total	84	100.0

*Not included in the calculation of percentages.

Table 8.22
Institutional investor characteristics—investment activity
The New Zealand survey

Amount of portfolio managed**		
	Number	Percentage
$1– $9,999	0	0.0
$10,000– $99,999	7	11.4
$100,000– $999,999	14	23.0
$1,000,000–$9,999,999	20	32.8
$10,000,000 and over	20	32.8
No information given	2*	
TOTAL	63	100.0

Amount of ordinary shares in portfolio		
	Number	Percentage
$1– $9,999	2	3.2
$10,000– $99,999	11	17.7
$100,000– $999,999	19	30.6
$1,000,000–$9,999,999	24	38.7
$10,000,000 and over	6	9.7
No information given	1*	
TOTAL	63	100.0

Trades made in the past year		
	Number	Percentage
None	3	4.9
1– 9	20	32.8
10–19	10	16.4
20–49	8	13.1
50 and over	20	32.8
No information given	2*	
TOTAL	63	100.0

*Not included in the calculation of percentages.

Table 8.23
Institutional investor characteristics—
Education, title, and experience of official responsible for investment decisions
The New Zealand survey

University degree in business	Number	Percentage
Yes	24	40.0
No	36	60.0
No information given	3*	
TOTAL	63	100.0

Title in firm	Number	Percentage
Company director	2	3.2
Finance director	6	9.7
Share officer or superannuation fund manager	4	6.5
Investment manager	11	17.7
General manager	9	14.5
Company secretary	16	25.8
Controller or chief accountant	6	9.7
Cost accountant	1	1.6
Research officer	1	1.6
Other titles	6	9.7
No information given	1*	
TOTAL	63	100.0

Experience in ordinary share investment	Number	Percentage
4 years or less	5	8.6
5– 9 years	16	27.6
10–19 years	19	32.8
20–39 years	17	29.3
40 years and over	1	1.7
No information given	5*	
TOTAL	63	100.0

*Not included in the calculation of percentages.

Table 8.24
Institutional investor characteristics—
Education and training of official responsible for investment decisions
The New Zealand survey

University degree in business		
	Number	Percentage
Yes	24	40.0
No	36	60.0
No information given	3*	___
TOTAL	63	100.0

Training in accounting		
Quarter hours	Number	Percentage
None	2	7.4
1–5	4	14.8
6–15	14	51.9
16–30	3	11.1
More than 30	4	14.8
No information given	36*	___
TOTAL	63	100.0

Training in finance, investment analysis, financial analysis, or stock market investing		
Quarter hours	Number	Percentage
None	2	8.7
1–5	7	30.4
6–15	10	43.5
16–30	4	17.4
More than 30	0	0.0
No information given	40*	___
TOTAL	63	100.0

*Not included in the calculation of percentages.

Table 8.25
Institutional investor characteristics—investment activity

Amount of portfolio managed			
	Percentage of respondents		
	U.S.	U.K.	N.Z.
$1– $9,999	0.6	0.0	0.0
$10,000– $99,999	4.6	2.1	11.4
$100,000– $999,999	11.0	0.0	23.0
$1,000,000–$9,999,999	16.3	10.4	32.8
$10,000,000 and over	67.5	87.5	32.8

Amount of common stock in portfolio			
	Percentage of respondents		
	U.S.	U.K.	N.Z.
$1– $9,999	1.9	0.0	3.2
$10,000– $99,999	7.1	2.1	17.7
$100,000– $999,999	15.5	0.0	30.6
$1,000,000–$9,999,999	22.6	8.3	38.7
$10,000,000 and over	52.9	89.6	9.7

Trades made in the previous year			
	Percentage of respondents		
	U.S.	U.K.	N.Z.
None	5.0	0.0	4.9
1– 9	15.1	0.0	32.8
10–19	20.1	2.1	16.4
20–49	13.9	4.3	13.1
50 and over	45.9	93.6	32.8

Table 8.26
Financial analyst characteristics—
Professional activity, experience, and education
The United Kingdom survey

Professional activity		
	Number	Percentage
Security analyst	54	79.4
Fund or money manager	0	0.0
Investment counselor	9	13.2
Other	5	7.4
No information given	6*	
TOTAL	74	100.0
Experience		
	Number	Percentage
4 years or less	6	8.1
5– 9 years	26	35.1
10–19 years	34	46.0
20–39 years	8	10.8
40 years and over	0	0.0
No information given	0	
TOTAL	74	100.0
University degree in business		
	Number	Percentage
Yes	36	50.0
No	36	50.0
No information given	2*	
TOTAL	74	100.0

*Not included in the calculation of percentages.

Table 8.27
Financial analyst characteristics—
Professional activity, experience, and education
The New Zealand survey

Professional activity	Number	Percentage
Security analyst	2	3.4
Fund or money manager	3	5.0
Investment counselor	38	63.3
Other	17	28.3
No information given	1*	
TOTAL	63	100.0

Experience	Number	Percentage
4 years or less	5	8.2
5– 9 years	8	13.1
10–19 years	21	34.4
20–39 years	23	37.7
40 years and over	4	6.6
No information given	0	
TOTAL	61	100.0

University degree in business	Number	Percentage
Yes	27	46.6
No	31	53.4
No information given	3*	
TOTAL	61	100.0

*Not included in the calculation of percentages.

Table 8.28
Financial analyst characteristics—
Professional activity, experience, and education

Professional activity	Percentage of respondents		
	U.S.	U.K.	N.Z.
Security analyst	34.1	79.4	3.4
Fund or money manager	35.0	0.0	5.0
Investment counselor	16.3	13.2	63.3
Other	14.6	7.4	28.3

Experience	Percentage of respondents		
	U.S.	U.K.	N.Z.
Under 4 years	4.1	8.1	8.2
5– 9 years	18.0	35.1	13.1
10–19 years	41.8	46.0	34.4
20–39 years	27.9	10.8	37.7
40 years and more	8.2	0.0	6.6

Education	Percentage of respondents		
	U.S.	U.K.	N.Z.
University degree in business			
Yes	85.4	50.0	46.6
No	14.6	50.0	53.4

Table 8.29
Institutional investors and financial analysts—
Education and training in accounting and finance
The United States survey

Education		
	Institutional investors	Financial analysts
	Percentage	Percentage
Degree in business	80.9	85.4
Other	19.1	14.6

Training in accounting		
	Institutional investors	Financial analysts
	Percentage	Percentage
Quarter hours:		
None	11.2	10.0
1– 5	7.7	14.6
6–15	37.0	33.6
16–30	24.5	31.8
More than 30	19.6	10.0

Training in finance and investment analysis		
	Institutional investors	Financial analysts
	Percentage	Percentage
Quarter hours:		
None	11.3	10.3
1– 5	5.6	5.6
6–15	36.6	35.5
16–30	24.6	29.9
More than 30	21.9	18.7

9 :: Classification of Individual Investors by Degree of Sophistication

In the literature on financial reporting, reference is often made to a user group called "sophisticated investors." Institutional investors and financial analysts belong in this group by any standards. The characteristics of these groups identified in chapter 8 confirm that their sophistication is a function of both the role they play in the world of investment, and the education, training, and experience they collectively have.

The question arises whether we can identify a stratum of individual investors who qualify as sophisticated investors. If so, then financial reports can be seen to conform to the FASB's assumption that

> Financial reporting should provide information that is useful to present and potential investors. . . . The information should be comprehensible to those who have a reasonable understanding of business and economic activities and are willing to study the information with reasonable diligence. (Statement of Financial Accounting Concepts No. 1, para. 34)

Characteristics of Individual Investors as Indicators of Sophistication

Using T-tests, we compared the investment objectives of individual investors with each of the ten characteristics listed in chapter 8, separately for the three national groups. Our objective was to find out if one or more characteristics could be used to identify those individual investors having short-term capital gains as their investment objective.

The Appendix to this chapter identifies the subgroups of individual investors designated 1A, 1B, etc. on tables 9.1 through 9.9. The tabulated data have been omitted for reasons of space. The results of these tests indicated a number of significant differences, and we attempted to find one characteristic, or even one type of characteristic (for instance, investment activity, personal characteristics, education) that could be said to identify the short-term trader.

Confining ourselves to the United States survey, we found the following people likely to pursue short-term capital gains:

—investors with small portfolios
—investors having fewer than ten years' investment ex-

perience and those reporting more than ten trades during the preceding year
—the over-50 age group
—investors with training in accounting, finance, or stock market investing

Because of the apparent relationships between some characteristics and the objective of short-term capital gains, we decided to test a new hypothesis, namely, that individual investors having the objectives of short-term capital gains would place less importance on financial reporting than other individual investors. The significance of this hypothesis lies in the observation that this subgroup of individual investors should not be regarded as part of the user group, and in its implications for the efficient market hypothesis (Mayer-Sommer 1979).

Assume a market with one security and 100 individual investors, of whom 50 are short-term traders and 50 long-term investors. In a period of time $\underline{t}$, a trader will make 5 trades. A long-term investor will hold the security an average of ten time periods (10 x $\underline{t}$). During any period $\underline{t}_0 \ldots . \underline{t}_n$ there will be 255 trades, 250 of which are the actions of traders, and 5 of which are the actions of individual investors. In such a market, the influence of financial report information on price or quantity of the security traded will be so small as to be imperceptible.

This assumption can be demonstrated graphically, using the formal model of price theory, thus:

Diagram 9.1. Formal Model of Price Theory

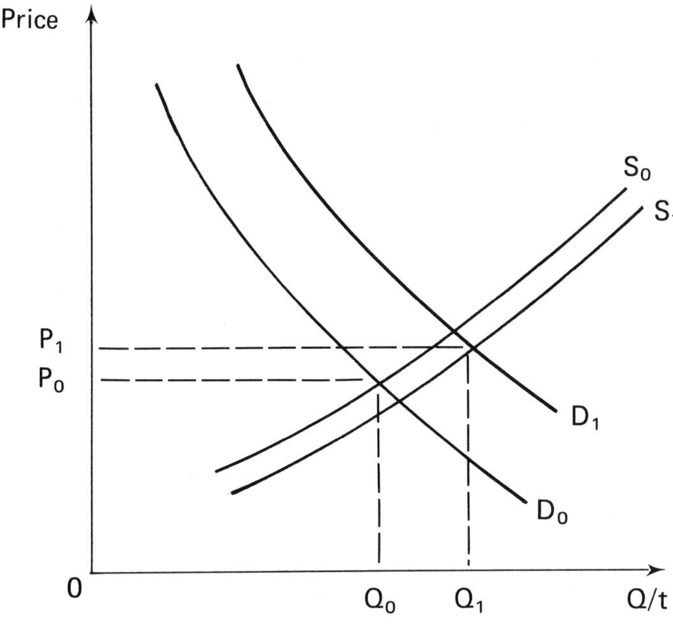

Diagram 9.2. Supply and Demand Curves of Mostly Short-Term Traders

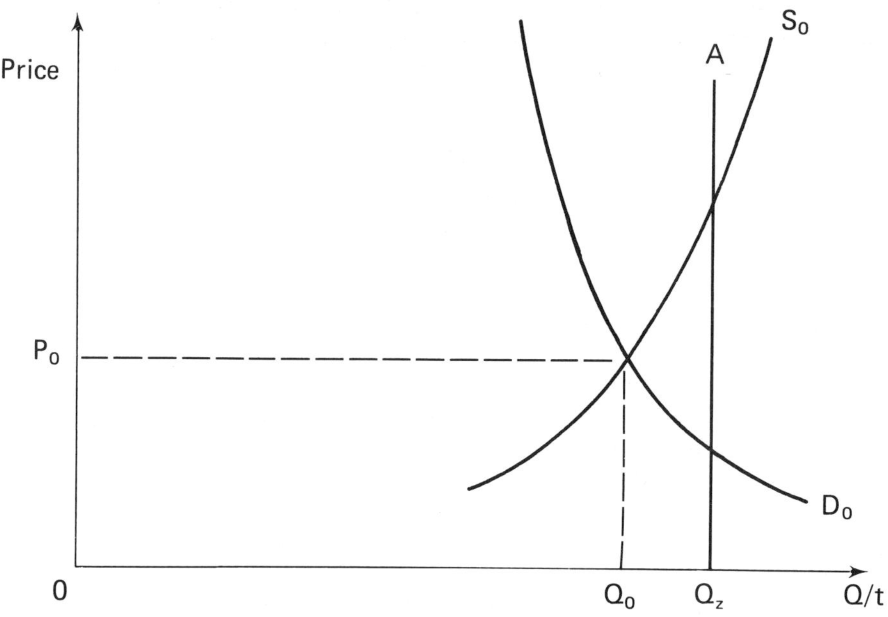

In the conventional presentation of the supply/demand equation at equilibrium, a quantity of security X (Q_0) is traded at a price P_0, which clears the market. New information, e.g., financial reporting, is received, causing the demand and supply functions to change. A new equilibrium is found at P_1 and Q_1 in Diagram 9.1.

In Diagram 9.2 we represent the market described, so that the demand and supply curves D_0 and S_0 are almost entirely composed of traders with short-term objectives. Now new information of an accounting nature, which by definition is of interest primarily to long-term holders, is disregarded by the traders. Long-term holders are represented by the fixed supply line AQ_z. They hold a quantity of the security comparable with that transacted by the traders; however, none of this quantity is on the market at a price P_0.

Classification by Investment Objectives

Following this hypothesis, we divided individual investors into two groups:

Group 1—Those rating short-term capital gains as important investment objectives.

Group 2—All other (i.e., those rating some other investment objective important).

The results of T-tests performed on the data indicate that the differences in the responses of the two groups with regard to the importance of various information sources were significant only with respect to

U.S. investors —stockbrokers' advice
—proxy statements
—advice of friends
—tips and rumors
U.K. investors —none
N.Z. investors —none

We see that both groups placed comparable importance on corporate annual reports as a source of investment information. It is relevant to our purpose, however, to observe that Group 1 rated stockbrokers' advice, advice of friends, and tips and rumors significantly higher than did Group 2.

We also noted that the differences in the responses of the two groups with regard to the importance of corporate annual report items were significant only with respect to

U.S. investors —president's letter (holding or selling only)
—pictorial material
—accounting policies (holding or selling only)
—sales and income by product line (holding or selling only)
U.K. investors —pictorial material
N.Z. investors —none

Both groups placed comparable importance on financial statement items as a source of investment information.

The results also show that the U.S. investors with short-term objectives rated the 10-K Report significantly more important than did the other investors with respect to holding or selling decisions. The additional importance of 10-K Reports to investors having short-term objectives must lie elsewhere than in the accounting data in those reports, which is available to the investors from corporate annual reports.

We concluded that our findings did not support the hypothesis that short-term investors place less importance on financial reporting. The result was surprising to us, and we attempted to investigate it by examining the questionnaires returned by individual investors in the U.S. surveys who had checked short-term capital gains as their most important investment objective.

We found that only four respondents checked this objective exclusively. All others rated several investment objectives important, including both short-term and long-term capital gains. This finding, that individual investors behave in several ways (i.e., both as traders and as investors) indicates that a model which seeks to represent a securities market must be more complex than we have previously believed. For example, the same individual may enter the market either as a trader or as a long-term investor, depending upon factors which are as yet unknown. (For a description of this process by a practicing psychologist, see Blotnick 1979: 144–45.)

Characteristics of Individual Investors and the Importance of Accounting Information

We attempted to find relationships between ten specific characteristics of individual investors and their ratings of information sources and corporate annual report items. T-tests were performed between all characteristics and ratings of information sources for individual investors in the United States, the United Kingdom, and New Zealand. The results displayed in tables 9.1 through 9.3 indicate that few significant differences emerged.

T-tests were performed between characteristics and ratings of corporate annual report items for individual investors in the three countries. Tables 9.4 through 9.6 show the statistically significant differences that emerged. It appears that U.S. individual

Table 9.1
Significant differences between individual investors' characteristics
and perceived importance of information sources
The United States survey

	Characteristics									
Information sources	SP	CS	IE	NT	AG	AI	OC	LE	MC	IT
Stockbrokers' advice										
Advisory services				*4B						
Corporate annual reports								**8A		
Newspapers and magazines										
Proxy statements										
Advice of friends	*1A									
Tips and rumors	**1A				**5A					

*Significant at level of 0.05.
**Significant at levels of 0.05 and 0.01.

Key to Column Heads

SP:	Size of portfolio	AI:	Annual income
CS:	Common stock investment in portfolio	OC:	Occupation
IE:	Investment experience	LE:	Level of education
NT:	Number of trades made	MC:	Major in college
AG:	Age	IT:	Formal investment training

Table 9.2
Significant differences between individual investors' characteristics
and perceived importance of information sources
The United Kingdom survey

	Characteristics						
Information sources	Size of portfolio	Ordinary share investment in portfolio	Investment experience	Number of trades made	Age	Annual income	Occupation
Sharebrokers' advice							
Advisory services							
Company annual reports							
Newspapers and magazines							*7A
Published statements by company directors					*5B		*7A
Advice of friends							
Tips and rumors							

*Significant at level of 0.05.
**Significant at levels of 0.05 and 0.01.

Table 9.3
Significant differences between individual investors' characteristics
and perceived importance of information sources
The New Zealand survey

	Characteristics						
Information sources	Size of portfolio	Ordinary share investment in portfolio	Investment experience	Number of trades made	Age	Annual income	Occupation
Sharebrokers' advice							
Advisory services		**2B		**4B			
Company annual reports							
Newspapers and magazines							
Published statements by company directors							
Advice of friends							*7A
Tips and rumors							

*Significant at level of 0.05.
**Significant at levels of 0.05 and 0.01.

investors' views on the importance of corporate annual report items were highly correlated with occupation, major in college, and amount of formal investment training. In all cases, investors having a major in accounting or business administration, an investment-related occupation, and/or training in accounting, finance, or investment, rated financial statement parts of the corporate annual report higher than did other individual investors.

Table 9.4
Significant differences between individual investors' characteristics
and perceived importance of corporate annual report items
The United States survey

	Characteristics									
Corporate annual report items	SP	CS	IE	NT	AG	AI	OC	LE	MC	IT
President's letter										
Buying decisions		*2B	**3B			*6B				
Holding or selling decisions			*3B							
Pictorial material										
Buying decisions						*6A				
Holding or selling decisions										
Balance sheet										
Buying decisions							**7A		*9A	*10A
Holding or selling decisions							*7A			
Income statement										
Buying decisions		*2B					*7A		**9A	*10A
Holding or selling decisions	*1B						*7A		**9A	*10A
Statement of changes in financial position										
Buying decisions								*8A		
Holding or selling decisions										
Accounting policies										
Buying decisions							**7A		**9A	**10A
Holding or selling decisions							*7A		**9A	**10A
Other footnotes										
Buying decisions						*6B	**7A		**9A	**10A
Holding or selling decisions						*6B	**7A		**9A	**10A
Auditor's report										
Buying decisions							**7A			
Holding or selling decisions							**7A		**9A	
Summary of operations for the last 5–10 years										
Buying decisions	*1B			*4B	*5B					
Holding or selling decisions					*5B					
Managment's discussion and analysis of the summary of operations										
Buying decisions										
Holding or selling decisions										
Sales and income by product line										
Buying decisions					**5A				**9A	*10A
Holding or selling decisions					*5A					
Form 10-K report										
Buying decisions					*5A		**7A		*9A	*10A
Holding or selling decisions							**7A			*10A

*Significant at level of 0.05.
**Significant at levels of 0.05 and 0.01.

KEY TO COLUMN HEADS

SP:	Size of portfolio	AI:	Annual income
CS:	Common stock investment in portfolio	OC:	Occupation
IE:	Investment experience	LE:	Level of education
NT:	Number of trades made	MC:	Major in college
AG:	Age	IT:	Formal investment training

Table 9.5
Significant differences between individual investors' characteristics
and perceived importance of corporate annual report items
The United Kingdom survey

	Characteristics							
Company annual report items	SP	OR	IE	NT	AG	AI	OC	IT
Chairman's letter								
Buying decisions								
Holding or selling decisions								
Pictorial material								
Buying decisions								
Holding or selling decisions								
Balance sheet								
Buying decisions								**10A
Holding or selling decisions						*6B		**10A
Profit and loss account								
Buying decisions						*6B	*7A	**10A
Holding or selling decisions	*1B					**6B	**7A	**10A
Statement of changes in financial position								
Buying decisions								
Holding or selling decisions	*1B					*6B	**7A	
Accounting policies								
Buying decisions							**7A	*10A
Holding or selling decisions							**7A	*10A
Other footnotes								
Buying decisions								
Holding or selling decisions								
Auditor's report								
Buying decisions								*10A
Holding or selling decisions								
Summary of operations for the last 5–10 years								
Buying decisions					*5B			
Holding or selling decisions								
Management's discussion and analysis of the summary of operations								
Buying decisions	**1B						*7A	
Holding or selling decisions								
Sales and profits by product line								
Buying decisions								
Holding or selling decisions								
Annual return filed with registrar of companies								
Buying decisions								
Holding or selling decisions								

*Significant at level of 0.05.
**Significant at levels of 0.05 and 0.01.

Key to Column Heads

SP:	Size of portfolio	AG:	Age
OR:	Ordinary share investment in portfolio	AI:	Annual income
IE:	Investment experience	OC:	Occupation
NT:	Number of trades made	IT:	Formal investment training

Table 9.6
Significant differences between individual investors' characteristics and perceived importance of corporate annual report items
The New Zealand survey

Company annual report items	Characteristics							
	SP	OR	IE	NT	AG	AI	OC	LE
Chairman's letter								
Buying decisions					*5B			
Holding or selling decisions								
Pictorial material								
Buying decisions								
Holding or selling decisions			*3B					
Balance sheet								
Buying decisions								*8A
Holding or selling decisions								**8A
Profit and loss account								
Buying decisions								
Holding or selling decisions								
Statement of changes in financial position								
Buying decisions								
Holding or selling decisions								
Accounting policies								
Buying decisions								
Holding or selling decisions								*8A
Other footnotes								
Buying decisions								
Holding or selling decisions								*8A
Auditor's report								
Buying decisions								
Holding or selling decisions						*6A		*8A
Summary of operations for the last 5–10 years								
Buying decisions								
Holding or selling decisions								
Management's discussion and analysis of the summary of operations								
Buying decisions								
Holding or selling decisions								
Sales and profits by product line								
Buying decisions								**8A
Holding or selling decisions								**8A
Annual return filed by registrar of companies								
Buying decisions								
Holding or selling decisions								

*Significant at level of 0.05.
**Significant at levels of 0.05 and 0.01.

KEY TO COLUMN HEADS

SP:	Size of portfolio	AG:	Age
OR:	Ordinary share investment in portfolio	AI:	Annual income
IE:	Investment experience	OC:	Occupation
NT:	Number of trades made	LE:	Level of education

This observation was only partially true for U.K. individual investors. Only eight of the ten characteristics were tested for this user group because of insufficient numbers of one or the other of the groups to test the relationship for the remaining two characteristics. There were significant differences confirming the U.S. results with respect to occupation and formal investment training. The N.Z. results were affected by the lack of information about characteristics in many of the questionnaires returned, but they confirmed the U.K. findings.

It might be supposed that sophisticated individual investors would be more likely to view forecasts of corporate performance as important than would the unsophisticated. We therefore attempted to find relationships between characteristics of individual investors and ratings of the importance of forecasted financial information.

T-tests were performed for this purpose, separately for U.S., U.K., and N.Z. individual investors and distinguishing between responses relating to "buy" and "hold/sell" decisions. The significant relationships are displayed in tables 9.7 through 9.9.

Briefly, the U.S. individual investors with smaller common stock portfolios (under $50,000) placed more importance on forecast sales, cost of goods sold, expenses, earnings, and cash flow than did those with larger portfolios. U.K. individual investors with investment-related occupations placed more importance on these same items except expenses, and also on additions to plant and equipment. Both groups rated buy decisions virtually the same as hold/sell decisions. There were insufficient significant differences among N.Z. individual investors to warrant conclusions.

It appears, therefore, that degrees of sophistication could not be determined on the basis of views on the importance of forecasts.

Sophisticated Individual Investors

Still with the objective of discovering a subgroup of sophisticated individual investors, we hypothesized that individual investors having educational and professional backgrounds similar to those of institutional investors and financial analysts would tend to resemble the latter two groups in their views of the importance of corporate annual reports and financial statements.

Following this hypothesis we divided the U.S. individual investors into two groups:

Group 1—those resembling institutional investors and financial analysts in

(a) having majored in college in accounting or business administration;

Table 9.7
Significant differences between individual investors' characteristics
and perceived usefulness of forecast financial information
The United States survey

Forecast items	Characteristics									
	SP	CS	IE	NT	AG	AI	OC	LE	MC	IT
Sales revenue										
Buying decisions		**2A								
Holding or selling decisions		**2A								
Cost of goods sold forecast for next year										
Buying decisions	**1A.	**2A.	**3A							
Holding or selling decisions	**1A.	**2A.	**3A.		*5A					
Expenses forecast for next year										
Buying decisions	*1A.	**2A.	*3A							
Holding or selling decisions	**1A.	**2A.				*6A				
Earnings forecast for next year										
Buying decisions	*1A.	**2A								
Holding or selling decisions	**1A.	**2A								
Cash flow forecast for next year										
Buying decisions	**1A.	*2A								
Holding or selling decisions	*1A.	*2A								
Dividends forecast for next year										
Buying decisions					**5B.	**6A.				**10B
Holding or selling decisions					**5B.	**6A.				**10B
Additions to plant and equipment forecast for next year										
Buying decisions	*1A.			*4A.			*7A			
Holding or selling decisions							*7A			

*Significant at level of 0.05.
**Significant at levels of 0.05 and 0.01.

KEY TO COLUMN HEADS

SP: Size of portfolio
CS: Common stock investment in portfolio
IE: Investment experience
NT: Number of trades made
AG: Age
AI: Annual income
OC: Occupation
LE: Level of education
MC: Major in college
IT: Formal investment training

(b) reporting formal education or training in accounting, finance, or stock market investing;
(c) having an investment-related occupation.

Group 2—all others (the unsophisticated subgroup).

There was no significant difference between Group 1 and institutional investors with respect to any of the investment objectives listed in the questionnaire.

We then compared the responses to the question on information sources of Group 1 with responses of institutional investors and financial analysts. The T-tests disclosed that

Table 9.8
Significant differences between individual investors' characteristics and perceived usefulness of forecast financial information
The United Kingdom survey

Forecast items	Characteristics							
	SP	OR	IE	NT	AG	AI	OC	IT
Sales revenue forecast for next year								
Buying decisions							*7A	
Holding or selling decisions							**7A	
Cost of goods sold forecast for next year								
Buying decisions				*4B			**7A	*8A
Holding or selling decisions							**7A	
Expenses forecast for next year								
Buying decisions								
Holding or selling decisions								
Earnings forecast for next year								
Buying decisions							*7A	
Holding or selling decisions							*7A	
Cash flow forecast for next year								
Buying decisions						*6B	**7A	
Holding or selling decisions							*7A	
Dividends forecast for next year								
Buying decisions								
Holding or selling decisions								
Additions to plant and equipment forecast for next year								
Buying decisions							*7A	
Holding or selling decisions							*7A	

*Significant at level of 0.05.
**Significant at levels of 0.05 and 0.01.

KEY TO COLUMN HEADS

SP:	Size of portfolio	AG:	Age
OR:	Ordinary share investment in portfolio	AI:	Annual income
IE:	Investment experience	OC:	Occupation
NT:	Number of trades made	IT:	Formal investment training

—Group 1 rated newspapers and magazines more important than did institutional investors.

—Group 1 rated stockbrokers' advice and advice of friends more important than did institutional investors.

—Financial analysts rated corporate annual reports and proxy statements more important than did Group 1.

We then compared the responses on the importance of corporate annual report items of Group 1 individual investors with institutional investors and financial analysts, separately for buy-

Table 9.9
Significant differences between individual investors' characteristics
and perceived usefulness of forecast financial information
The New Zealand survey

	Characteristics							
Forecast items	SP	OR	IE	NT	AG	AI	OC	LE
Sales revenue forecast for next year								
Buying decisions							*7A	
Holding or selling decisions								
Cost of goods sold forecast for next year								
Buying decisions	**1A		*3A		*5A			
Holding or selling decisions	*1A				*5A			
Expenses forecast for next year								
Buying decisions								
Holding or selling decisions					*5A			
Earnings forecast for next year								
Buying decisions								
Holding or selling decisions								
Cash flow forecast for next year								
Buying decisions								
Holding or selling decisions			*3A					
Dividends forecast for next year								
Buying decisions								
Holding or selling decisions								
Additions to plant and equipment forecast for next year								
Buying decisions								
Holding or selling decisions								

*Significant at level of 0.05.
**Significant at levels of 0.05 and 0.01.

KEY TO COLUMN HEADS

SP:	Size of portfolio	AG:	Age
OR:	Ordinary share investment in portfolio	AI:	Annual income
IE:	Investment experience	OC:	Occupation
NT:	Number of trades made	LE:	Level of education

ing and hold/sell decisions. Table 9.10 shows that there were significant differences between Group 1 and the two professional groups on the majority of items.

There were also significant differences between Group 1 and the two professional groups with respect to use of the 10-K Report, which Group 1 used less. There was no significant difference with respect to interim financial statements. Only three significant differences emerged between Group 1 and financial analysts with regard to views on the usefulness of forecast information.

We regard the results of these tests as inconclusive and believe that they provide no support to our hypothesis.

Table 9.10
Significant differences between United States sophisticated investor groups with respect to corporate annual report items

GROUP 1 RATED SIGNIFICANTLY LOWER THAN INSTITUTIONAL INVESTORS
Balance sheet
Income statement (hold/sell only)
Statement of changes in financial position
Accounting policies
Other footnotes
Auditor's report
Management's discussion and analysis of summary operations (hold/sell only)
Sales and income by product line
10-K report

GROUP 1 RATED SIGNIFICANTLY LOWER THAN FINANCIAL ANALYSTS
President's letter
Balance sheet
Income statement
Statement of changes in financial position (buy only)
Accounting policies
Other footnotes
Auditor's report (buy only)
Management's discussion and analysis of summary of operations
Sales and income by product line
10-K report

Further Analysis of Sophisticated Individual Investors

The attempt to identify a sophisticated subgroup of individual investors was continued by an effort to find one of the three criteria (major in college; education in accounting or finance; investment-related occupation) that could be used as a surrogate for sophistication. Using T-tests, many significant differences emerged, so that the results were again inconclusive. There were fewer differences between individual investors with investment-related occupations and the two professional groups, a result which might have been expected. This finding suggests that further research on individual investors' uses of financial reporting should concentrate on the subgroup having investment-related occupations.

Extensive analyses of a similar kind were conducted on the U.K. and N.Z. data, leading to a similar conclusion. A subgroup of sophisticated individual investors could only be found by using investment-related occupation as the surrogate for sophistication.

Conclusion

We believe that we have succeeded in identifying a stratum of individual investors that may be characterized as sophisticated and included in the group of users of financial statements. This subgroup includes accountants, senior corporate executives and other management types, financial personnel, and business educators.

The results of this investigation are important for the evaluation of other surveys and security market research aimed at determining the importance of financial reporting for investment decisions. To the extent that surveys do not discriminate between sophisticated and unsophisticated users, the findings may be heavily weighted with the responses of nonusers. Similarly, if security market prices are largely the consequence of the operations of unsophisticated (nonuser) individual investors, the effect of accounting information is likely to be submerged in a mass of other factors, from which it is to be extracted with great difficulty, if at all.

:: Appendix to Chapter 9: Individual Investors Subgroups Used for T-Tests

1A. U.S. individual investors holding a portfolio of less than $50,000 (U.K.: less than £50,000; N.Z.: less than $10,000).

1B. U.S. individual investors holding a portfolio of $50,000 or more (U.K.: £5,000 or more; N.Z.: $10,000 or more).

2A. U.S. individual investors whose common stock investment in portfolio was less than $50,000 (U.K.: less than £5,000; N.Z.: less than $10,000).

2B. U.S. individual investors whose common stock investment in portfolio was $50,000 or over (U.K.: £5,000 or more; N.Z.: $10,000 or more).

3A. U.S. individual investors whose experience in common stock investment was less than 5 years (U.K.: less than 20 years; N.Z.: less than 10 years).

3B. U.S. individual investors whose experience in common stock investment was 5 years or longer (U.K.: 20 years or longer; N.Z.: 10 years or longer).

4A. U.S. individual investors who made fewer than 10 trades in the previous 12 months (U.K.: no trades; N.Z.: fewer than 10 trades).

4B. U.S. individual investors who made 10 or more trades in the previous 12 months (U.K.: one or more trades; N.Z.: 10 or more trades).

5A. U.S. individual investors who were 50 years old or younger.

5B. U.S. individual investors who were over 50 years old.

6A. U.S. individual investors whose annual income was less than $40,000 (U.K. less than £6,000; N.Z.: less than $10,000).

6B. U.S. individual investors whose annual income was $40,000 or more (U.K.: £6,000 or more; N.Z.: $10,000 or more).

7A. U.S. individual investors whose occupation was investment oriented.

7B. U.S. individual investors whose occupation was not investment oriented.

8A. U.S. individual investors who did not graduate from college.

8B. U.S. individual investors who graduated from college.

9A. U.S. individual investors whose major in college was accounting or business administration.

9B. U.S. individual investors whose major in college was not accounting or business administration or who did not attend college.

10A. U.S. individual investors who had no formal training in accounting, finance, or stock market investing.

:: Bibliography

Books and Monographs

Accounting Principles Board. "Basic Concepts and Accounting Principles Underlying Financial Statements of Business Enterprise." *Statement No. 4.* New York: American Institute of Certified Public Accountants, October 1970.

American Accounting Association Committee to Prepare a Statement of Basic Accounting Theory. *A Statement of Basic Accounting Theory.* Evanston, Ill.: AAA, 1966.

American Accounting Association Subcommittee on Establishing Materiality Criteria of the Committee on Financial Accounting Standards. "Response to the Financial Accounting Standards Board's Discussion Memorandum Entitled 'An Analysis of Issues Related to Criteria for Determining Materiality.'" *The Accounting Review* (supp. to vol. 52), 1976.

American Institute of Certified Public Accountants. *Establishing Financial Accounting Standards.* New York: AICPA, March 1972.

Arthur Andersen and Co. *Public Accounting in Transition.* Survey and report for Arthur Andersen and Co. by Opinion Research Corporation. Arthur Andersen and Co., 1974.

Chang, Lucia S., and Kenneth S. Most. *The Importance of Financial Statements for Investment Decisions: An Empirical Study of Investor Views.* Miami: Florida International University, 1978.

Duff and Phelps, Inc. *A Management Guide to Better Financial Reporting.* Arthur Andersen and Co., 1976.

Epstein, Marc H. *The Usefulness of Annual Reports to Corporate Shareholders.* Los Angeles: Bureau of Business and Economic Research, California State University, 1975.

Financial Accounting Standards Board. "Objectives of Financial Reporting by Business Enterprises." *Statement of Financial Accounting Concepts No. 1.* Stamford, Connecticut: FASB, November 1978.

______. *Tentative Conclusions on Objectives of Financial Statements of Business Enterprises.* Stamford, Connecticut: FASB, December 1976.

Financial Analysts Federation, The *Objective of Financial Accounting and Reporting from the Viewpoint of the Financial Analyst.* Statement to the AICPA Accounting Objectives Study Group by Financial Accounting Policy Committee, 30 March 1972.

Hawkins, David F., and Walter J. Campbell. *Equity Valuation Models: Analysis and Implications.* New York: Financial Executives Research Foundation, 1978.

Littleton, A. C. *Statement of Accounting Theory.* Evanston, Ill.: American Accounting Association, 1953.

Mattessich, Richard. *Accounting and Analytical Methods.* Homewood, Ill.: Richard D. Irwin, 1964.

Mautz, R. K. *Financial Reportion by Diversified Companies.* New York: Financial Executives Research Foundation, 1968.

Paton, W. H., and A. C. Littleton. *An Introduction to Corporate Accounting Standards.* American Accounting Association, 1940.

Price Waterhouse and Co. *The Objectives of Financial Statements.* New York: Price Waterhouse and Co., 1971.

Rao, Vasudeva. "An Analysis of Accounting Information Needs of Selected Users of Financial Statements." Unpublished doctoral dissertation, Texas A&M University, College Station, Texas, 1974.

Report of the Advisory Committee on Corporate Disclosure to the Securities and Exchange Commission. Washington, D.C.: U.S. Government Printing Office, 1977.

Rice, C. D. *Businessman's View of the Purposes of Financial Reporting.* New York: Financial Executives Research Foundation, 1973.

Staubus, George. *A Theory of Accounting to Investors.* Berkeley and Los Angeles: University of California Press, 1961.

Stockholders of America, Inc., *A Stockholders of America Survey on Subjects of Concern to the Individual Investor.* Washington, D.C.: Stockholders of America, Inc., 1975.

Study Group on the Objectives of Financial Statements. *Objectives of Financial Statements.* New York: American Institute of Certified Public Accountants, October 1973.

Articles

American Accounting Association Subcommittee on Establishing Materiality Criteria of the Committee on Financial Accounting Standards, "Response to the Financial Accounting Standards Board's Discussion Memorandum Entitled 'An Analysis of Issues Related Criteria for Determining Materiality.'" *The Accounting Review, Supplement to Vol. 52,* 1976.

Andersen, Corliss D., "The Financial Analyst's Needs," *Berkeley Symposium on the Foundations of Financial Accounting,* Berkeley: University of California, 1967, pp. 98–109.

Backer, Morton, "Financial Reporting and Security Investment Decisions," *Financial Executive,* December 1966, pp. 50–60.

Baker, Kent H., and John A. Haslem. "Information Needs of Individual Investors," *Journal of Accountancy,* November, 1973, pp. 64–69.

Benston, George J. "Evaluation of the Securities Exchange Act of 1934," *Financial Executive*, May, 1974, pp. 28–42.

Blotnick, Srully, "Will History Repeat?" *Forbes*, April 3, 1979, pp. 144–45.

Bradish, Richard D., "Corporate Reporting and the Financial Analysts," *The Accounting Review*, October 1965, pp. 755–66.

Brenner, Vincent C., "Financial Statement Users' Views of the Desirability of Reporting Current Cost Information," *Journal of Accounting Research*, Autumn, 1970, pp. 159–66.

Briggs, Douglas H., "Information Requirements of Users of Published Corporate Reports—Unit Trust," *Accounting and Business Research*, Winter 1975, pp. 14–23.

Buzby, Stephen L. "The Nature of Adequate Disclosure," *Journal of Accountancy*, April 1975, pp. 38–47.

Carlson, Arthur, "Corporate Reporting—A Security Analyst's Views," *Financial Executive*, May 1975, pp. 58–59.

Chandra, Gyan, "A Study of the Consensus on Disclosure Among Public Accountants and Security Analysts," *The Accounting Review*, October 1974, pp. 733–42.

Estes, Ralph W., "An Assessment of the Usefulness of Current Cost and Price-Level Information by Financial Statement Users," *The Journal of Accounting Research*, Autumn 1968, pp. 200–209.

Garrett, Ray Jr., "Disclosure Rules and Annual Reports: Present Impact," *Financial Executive*, April 1975.

Girdler, Reynolds, "18,000,000 Books Nobody Reads," *Saturday Review*, April 13, 1963.

Greer, Howard C. "The Corporation Stockholder—Accounting's Forgotten Man." *Accounting Review*, January 1964, pp. 22–31.

Lee, T.A., and D.P. Tweedie. "Accounting Information: An Investigation of Private Shareholder Usage," *Accounting and Business Research*, Autumn 1975, pp. 280–89; and "Accounting Information: An Investigation of Private Shareholder Understanding," *Accounting and Business Research*, Winter 1975, pp. 3–17.

Mayer-Sommer, Alan P., "Understanding and Acceptance of the Efficient Markets Hypothesis and its Accounting Implications," *Accounting Review*, January 1979, pp. 88–106.

Norr, David, "What a Financial Analyst Wants from an Annual Report," *Financial Executive*, August 1970, pp. 20–23.

Pankoff, Lyn D. and Robert L. Virgil, "Some Preliminary Findings from a Laboratory Experiment on the Usefulness of Financial Accounting Information to Security Analysts," *Empirical Research in Accounting: Selected Studies, 1970*. University of Chicago, 1970.

Trevelow, Rosemarie, "How a Security Analyst Uses the Annual Report," *Financial Executive*, November 1971, pp. 18–21.